Taste of Home's

GRILLING
RECIPE COLLECTION

Welcome to the Recipe Collection That's Really Sizzling!

GRILLING is a great way to prepare meals, whatever the season. After all, what other cooking method leaves you with a clean kitchen *and* especially flavorful fare to serve your family?

If just looking at the foods pictured in this *Taste of Home's Grilling Recipe Collection* makes your mouth start to water, wait until you get any of the 181 recipes cooking on the grill!

From beef, poultry, fish and pork entrees to side dishes, breads and even desserts, this cookbook offers a wide variety of recipes you can "cook out" with throughout the year.

Fellow grilling enthusiasts from across the country shared these great recipes, which have appeared in past issues of *Taste of Home* magazine and its "sister" publi-cations. Our home economists prepared and taste-tested each dish, compiling the best ones into this recipe collection.

Before you step outside and fire up the grill, though, check out the "Guide to Grilling" on pages 4 and 5. There you'll find all you need to know about the two grilling methods—direct and indirect—plus how to test the temperature of a charcoal grill. There's also a handy chart listing the cooking times for common grilled foods.

You're sure to appreciate these easy-to-follow techniques as well as the handy tips and hints we've sprinkled throughout the rest of the cookbook.

Suddenly in the mood for something flame-broiled? With *Taste of Home's Grilling Recipe Collection*, dinner will be sizzling in no time!

Editor: Jean Steiner
Art Director: Catherine Fletcher
Associate Editors: Julie Schnittka, Susan Uphill
Food Editor: Janaan Cunningham
Associate Food Editors: Coleen Martin, Diane Werner
Senior Recipe Editor: Sue A. Jurack
Recipe Editor: Janet Briggs
Food Photography: Rob Hagen, Dan Roberts
Senior Food Photography Artist: Stephanie Marchese
Food Photography Artist: Julie Ferron
Photo Studio Manager: Anne Schimmel
Chairman and Founder: Roy Reiman
President: Russell Denson

© 2004 Reiman Media Group, Inc.
5400 S. 60th St., Greendale WI 53129
International Standard Book Number: 0-89821-386-X
Library of Congress Control Number: 2003097390
All rights reserved.
Printed in U.S.A.

PICTURED ON COVER. Clockwise from top: Barbecued Spareribs (p. 53), Grilled Cheese Loaf (p. 94), Marinated Catfish Fillets (p. 74) and Pork with Tangy Mustard Sauce (p. 54).

CONTENTS

Taste of Home's Grilling Recipe Collection

p. 36

p.16

p. 97

p. 58

p. 75

p.106

Guide to Grilling

CHARCOAL and gas grill owners can choose from two cooking methods: direct and indirect grilling. Consult the manufacturer's instructions for details about your specific grill and follow these general guidelines:

The direct grilling method is what you likely use when cooking hot dogs and hamburgers. Simply put, food is cooked directly over an even heat source

cooking, foods do not need to be turned.

Often a combination of both methods is used. For example, a 1-1/2-inch-thick steak can be seared over direct heat for a short period of time and moved to the indirect heat area to continue cooking without excess browning.

For the best results, it's important to preheat your grill to the correct temperature for the type of food

A) Direct Grilling

B) Indirect Grilling

(see illustration A). The food is turned halfway through the cooking time to expose both sides to the heat. Covering the grill is optional with this method.

The direct grilling method is best for foods that take less than 30 minutes to cook, such as most steaks, pork chops, boneless chicken breasts and delicate vegetables.

With the indirect grilling method, foods are not cooked directly over the heat. On a charcoal grill, the hot coals are moved or "banked" to opposite sides of the grill, and a shallow foil pan is placed between the coals to catch the drippings (see illustration B). The food is placed on the center of the grill rack.

On a gas grill, the center burner or one of the side burners is turned off after the grill preheats. A shallow foil pan can be placed on the grill rack. Meats need to be elevated above the bottom of the pan with a roast rack or holder.

The indirect grilling method is a slower cooking method and is used for meats and vegetables that take longer than 30 minutes to cook, such as thick steaks, bone-in chicken parts, roasts, whole poultry, fresh sausage and solid vegetables. Because of the slower

you're cooking.

To test the temperature of a charcoal grill, cautiously hold your hand 4 inches over the coals. Count the seconds you can hold your hand in place before the heat forces you to pull away.

• **Hot:** The charcoal coals will glow red and you can hold your hand above the fire for no more than 2 seconds. For a gas grill, the temperature will read about 500°.

• **Medium-hot:** The coals are gray with a red underglow and you can hold your hand above the coals for no more than 3 seconds. For a gas grill, the temperature will read about 400°.

• **Medium:** The coals are gray with only a hint of red and you can hold your hand above the coals for no more than 4 seconds. For a gas grill, the temperature will read about 350°.

• **Low:** The coals are completely gray and you can hold your hand above the fire for 5 seconds. For a gas grill, the temperature will read about 300°.

Refer to the Grilling Guidelines chart at right for basic information about the grilling methods and cooking times for common grilled fare.

GRILLING GUIDELINES

Food	Grilling Method/Heat	Approx. Total Cooking Time/Internal Temperature
Beef		
Steak (3/4 to 1 inch thick)	Direct/Hot heat	6-7 minutes for rare (140°) 7-9 minutes for medium (160°) 9-11 minutes for well-done (170°)
Steak (1-1/2 inches thick)	Sear Direct/Medium-hot heat Cook Indirect/Medium heat	10-12 minutes for rare (140°) 12-15 minutes for medium (160°) 15-19 minutes for well-done (170°)
Ground Beef Patties (each 1/4 pound and 3/4 inch thick)	Direct/Medium-hot heat	11-13 minutes or until meat thermometer reads 160° and meat is no longer pink
Pork		
Tenderloin, whole (3/4 to 1 pound)	Direct/Medium heat	25-30 minutes or until meat thermometer reads 160°
Chops (3/4 to 1 inch thick)	Direct/Medium heat	25-30 minutes for medium (160°) 30-35 minutes for well-done (170°)
Hot Dogs	Direct/Medium-hot heat	6-10 minutes
Fresh Sausage	Indirect/Medium or Low heat	18-25 minutes or until meat thermometer reads 170°
Poultry		
Boneless Chicken Breasts (4 to 5 ounces each)	Direct/Medium-hot heat	10-14 minutes or until meat thermometer reads 170° and juices run clear
Chicken Parts (bone-in)	Indirect/Medium heat	50-60 minutes or until meat thermometer reads 170° (white meat) or 180° (dark meat) and juices run clear
Turkey Tenderloins (4 to 6 ounces each)	Direct/Medium-hot heat	10-12 minutes or until meat thermometer reads 170° and juices run clear

Beef and Ground Beef

Tender Flank Steak (p.15)

Chapter 1

Teriyaki Beef Kabobs

(Pictured below)

Lisa Hector, Estevan, Saskatchewan

Several years back, my sister-in-law brought this recipe on a family camping trip and we fixed it for an outdoor potluck. It was so delicious that I asked if I could have a copy to take home with me. It's become a summer standard for us ever since.

- 1/4 cup vegetable oil
- 1/4 cup orange juice
- 1/4 cup soy sauce
- 1 teaspoon garlic powder
- 1 teaspoon ground ginger
- 1-3/4 pounds beef tenderloin, cut into 1-inch cubes
- 3/4 pound cherry tomatoes
- 1/2 pound fresh whole mushrooms
- 2 large green peppers, cubed
- 1 large red onion, cut into wedges
- Hot cooked rice, optional

In a resealable plastic bag or shallow glass container, combine the first five ingredients and mix well. Reserve 1/2 cup for basting and refrigerate. Add beef to remaining marinade; turn to coat. Seal bag or cover container; refrigerate for 1 hour, turning occasionally. Drain and discard the marinade.

On metal or soaked wooden skewers, alternate beef, tomatoes, mushrooms, green peppers and onions. Grill, uncovered, over medium heat for 3 minutes on each side. Baste with reserved marinade. Continue turning and basting for 8-10 minutes or until meat reaches desired doneness. Serve meat and vegetables over rice if desired. **Yield:** 6-8 servings.

Decked-Out Burgers

(Pictured above)

Karen Bourne, Magrath, Alberta

This is an easy way to make ordinary burgers taste exceptionally good. Guests always enjoy the flavorful topping that's made with bacon, cheese, mushrooms and mayonnaise.

- 1 cup (4 ounces) shredded cheddar cheese
- 1 jar (4-1/2 ounces) sliced mushrooms, drained
- 1/3 cup mayonnaise

6 bacon strips, cooked and crumbled
1/4 cup finely chopped onion
1 teaspoon salt
1/2 teaspoon pepper
1/4 teaspoon garlic powder
1/8 teaspoon hot pepper sauce
1-1/2 pounds lean ground beef
6 hamburger buns, split
Lettuce leaves and tomato slices, optional

In a bowl, combine cheese, mushrooms, mayonnaise and bacon; cover and refrigerate. In another bowl, combine onion, salt, pepper, garlic powder and hot pepper sauce; add beef and mix well. Shape into six 1/2-in.-thick patties.

Grill, covered, over medium-hot heat for 4-5 minutes on each side. Spoon cheese mixture on top of each burger. Grill 1-2 minutes longer or until the cheese begins to melt. Serve on buns with lettuce and tomato if desired. **Yield:** 6 servings.

Grilled Beef Gyros

(Pictured at right)

Lee Rademaker, Hayfork, California

A spicy marinade adds zip to these grilled beef slices tucked inside pita bread. Friends from Greece gave us their recipe for the cucumber sauce, which provides a cool contrast to the hot beef.

1 medium onion, cut into chunks
2 garlic cloves
2 tablespoons sugar
1 tablespoon ground mustard
1/2 teaspoon ground ginger *or* 2 teaspoons minced fresh gingerroot
1-1/2 teaspoons pepper
1/2 teaspoon cayenne pepper
1/2 cup soy sauce
1/4 cup water
1 boneless beef sirloin tip roast (2 to 3 pounds), cut into 1/4-inch-thick slices
CUCUMBER SAUCE:
1 medium cucumber, peeled, seeded and cut into chunks
4 garlic cloves
1/2 teaspoon salt
1/3 cup cider vinegar

1/3 cup olive *or* vegetable oil
2 cups (16 ounces) sour cream
8 to 10 pita breads, warmed and halved
Thinly sliced onion
Chopped tomato

In a blender or food processor, place the onion, garlic, sugar, mustard, ginger, pepper and cayenne; cover and process until onion is finely chopped. Add soy sauce and water; process until blended. Place the beef in a large resealable plastic bag. Add marinade. Seal bag and turn to coat; refrigerate for 1-2 hours.

For sauce, combine the cucumber, garlic and salt in a blender or food processor; cover and process until cucumber is chopped. Add vinegar and oil; process until blended. Transfer to a bowl; stir in sour cream. Refrigerate until serving.

Drain and discard marinade. Grill beef, covered, over medium-hot heat until meat reaches desired doneness. Place beef in pita halves. Top with cucumber sauce, sliced onion and chopped tomato. Refrigerate any remaining sauce. **Yield:** 8-10 sandwiches.

juice, vinegar, oil, garlic, Worcestershire sauce, oregano, salt and pepper. Pour 1-1/2 cups over meat. Pour remaining marinade over vegetables. Cover and refrigerate overnight. Drain meat and vegetables, discarding marinade.

Grill steak, covered, over medium-hot heat for 10 minutes on each side or until meat reaches desired doneness (for rare, a meat thermometer should read 140°; medium, 160°; well-done, 170°).

Meanwhile, cut two pieces of heavy-duty foil into 18-in. x 12-in. rectangles. Wrap tortillas in one piece and vegetables in the other; seal foil tightly. Grill, covered, over indirect heat for 5-7 minutes, turning occasionally. Cut steak into 1/8-in. slices across the grain; place on tortillas. Top with vegetables and roll up. Serve with avocado and sour cream if desired. **Yield:** 6 servings.

Grilled Steak Fajitas

(Pictured above)

Pamela Pogue, Quitman, Texas

This tasty main dish is as quick and easy to assemble as tacos. Marinating the meat overnight makes it very tender. We like the hearty and flavorful steak slices. I serve the fajitas with Spanish rice and refried beans.

> 1 flank steak (1-1/2 pounds)
> 1 large onion, cut into wedges
> 1 medium green pepper, julienned
> 1 can (4 ounces) chopped green chilies
> 1/2 cup lemon juice
> 1/2 cup red wine vinegar *or* cider vinegar
> 1/2 cup vegetable oil
> 4 garlic cloves, minced
> 1 tablespoon Worcestershire sauce
> 1 teaspoon dried oregano
> 1/2 teaspoon salt
> 1/2 teaspoon pepper
> 12 flour tortillas (6 inches)
> 1 medium avocado, peeled and sliced, optional
> Sour cream, optional

Place steak in a shallow glass container or large resealable plastic bag. Place onion and green pepper in another container or bag. Combine chilies, lemon

Cool Kitchen Meat Loaf

(Pictured below)

Susan Taul, Birmingham, Alabama

Juicy slices of this tender meat loaf are wonderful served with a homemade sweet-and-sour sauce. It's an easy way to fix supper, especially when the weather is hot.

1 cup soft bread crumbs
1 medium onion, chopped
1/2 cup tomato sauce
1 egg
1-1/2 teaspoons salt
1/4 teaspoon pepper
1-1/2 pounds lean ground beef
SAUCE:
1/2 cup ketchup
3 tablespoons brown sugar
3 tablespoons Worcestershire sauce
2 tablespoons vinegar
2 tablespoons prepared mustard

In a bowl, combine the first six ingredients. Add beef and mix well. Shape into two loaves; place each loaf in a disposable 8-in. x 4-in. x 2-in. loaf pan. Cover with foil. Grill, covered, over indirect medium heat for 30 minutes or until the meat is no longer pink and a meat thermometer reads 160°.

Meanwhile, in a saucepan, combine the sauce ingredients. Cook and stir over low heat until sugar is dissolved. Spoon over meat loaves before serving. **Yield:** 2 loaves (3 servings each).

Blues Burgers

(Pictured above right)

Dee Dee Mitchell, Longmont, Colorado

If you like blue cheese, you'll love the flavorful surprise inside these moist hamburgers. They're so filling that just a serving of tangy coleslaw on the side makes for a hearty meal.

1/2 pound fresh mushrooms, sliced
2 tablespoons butter *or* margarine
1/2 teaspoon ground cumin
1/2 teaspoon paprika
1/4 teaspoon chili powder
1/4 teaspoon salt
1/4 teaspoon pepper
Pinch cayenne pepper
1-1/2 pounds lean ground beef
2 ounces crumbled blue cheese
2/3 cup barbecue sauce
4 onion rolls *or* hamburger buns, split

In a skillet, saute mushrooms in butter for 2-3 minutes or until tender. Set aside and keep warm. In a

bowl, combine the next six ingredients; add beef and mix well. Shape into eight thin patties. Sprinkle half of the patties with blue cheese. Place remaining patties on top and press edges firmly to seal. Grill, uncovered, over medium-hot heat for 3 minutes on each side. Brush with barbecue sauce.

Grill 10-12 minutes longer or until meat is no longer pink, basting and turning occasionally. Drain the mushrooms. Serve burgers on rolls topped with mushrooms. **Yield:** 4 servings.

Hamburger Know-How

WHEN MAKING hamburger patties, remember that the higher percentage of fat in ground meat, the more shrinkage there is after cooking. So if you're making hamburgers out of regular ground beef, form the patties so they're about 1/2 inch larger in diameter than the hamburger bun.

Place the patties on a sheet of waxed paper on a tray. Once you start grilling, just lift the corner of the waxed paper to easily remove them from the tray.

Herbed Beef Tenderloin

(Pictured below)

Paul Verner, Wooster, Ohio

Cooking on the grill has always been one of my favorite hobbies. This recipe is a popular choice for my family's Sunday suppers or our special birthday dinners. I like to serve tenderloin with baked potatoes and home-grown vegetables.

    1 beef tenderloin (4 to 5 pounds)
    2 garlic cloves, minced
    2 green onions, finely chopped
    1 tablespoon Dijon mustard
    1 tablespoon red wine vinegar *or* balsamic vinegar
1/2 cup olive *or* vegetable oil
    1 tablespoon *each* dried basil, thyme and rosemary, crushed
    1 teaspoon salt
    1 teaspoon pepper

Place tenderloin in a shallow glass container or resealable plastic bag. Combine remaining ingredients; pour over meat. Cover container or seal bag; refrigerate overnight, turning occasionally. Drain and discard the marinade.

Grill beef, uncovered, over medium-hot heat for 20 minutes, turning frequently. Cover and continue to grill for 10-20 minutes or until meat reaches desired doneness (for rare, a meat thermometer should read 140°; medium, 160°; well-done, 170°). Let stand 10 minutes before slicing. **Yield:** 8-10 servings.

Surprise Meatball Skewers

(Pictured above)

Kristen Wondra, Hudson, Kansas

I still remember the first time I served these colorful kabobs—my family was thrilled to find a surprise in the tasty meatballs. Since I make them often, I sometimes substitute different vegetables or cheeses for variety.

1/3 cup honey
    3 tablespoons Dijon mustard
    2 tablespoons finely chopped onion
    2 tablespoons apple juice *or* cider
Dash cayenne pepper
    1 egg
1/4 cup dry bread crumbs

1 tablespoon minced fresh parsley
1 teaspoon Italian seasoning
1/4 teaspoon salt
Pepper to taste
1 pound ground beef
1 block (1-1/2 ounces) Monterey Jack *or*
  Swiss cheese, cut into 12 cubes
12 small mushrooms, stems removed
1 medium green pepper, cut into pieces
1 medium sweet yellow *or* red pepper, cut
  into pieces
1 medium onion, cut into wedges

In a saucepan, combine the first five ingredients. Bring to a boil. Reduce heat; simmer, uncovered, for 5-7 minutes or until onion is tender and sauce is slightly thickened. Remove from the heat; set aside.

In a large bowl, combine the egg, bread crumbs, parsley, Italian seasoning, salt and pepper. Add beef and mix well. Divide into 12 portions. Place a cube of cheese in each mushroom cap; shape each meat portion around a mushroom.

On six metal or soaked wooden skewers, alternate meatballs, peppers and onion wedges. Grill, uncovered, over medium heat for 3 minutes on each side. Grill 10-12 minutes longer or until meat is no longer pink, turning occasionally. Brush with reserved glaze during the last 2 minutes. **Yield:** 6 servings.

Cajun Burgers

(Pictured below left)

Julie Culbertson, Bensalem, Pennsylvania

My family likes spicy food. I found the original recipe for these burgers in a cookbook, then added and subtracted ingredients until they suited our taste. They are always on the menu whenever we cook out.

CAJUN SEASONING BLEND:
3 tablespoons ground cumin
3 tablespoons dried oregano
1 tablespoon garlic powder
1 tablespoon paprika
2 teaspoons salt
1 teaspoon cayenne pepper
BURGERS:
1/4 cup finely chopped onion
1 teaspoon salt
1 teaspoon Cajun Seasoning Blend
  (recipe above)
1/2 to 1 teaspoon hot pepper sauce
1/2 teaspoon dried thyme
1/4 teaspoon dried basil
1 garlic clove, minced
1 pound ground beef
4 hamburger buns, split
Sauteed onions, optional

Combine all seasoning blend ingredients in a small bowl or resealable plastic bag; mix well. In a bowl, combine the first seven burger ingredients; add beef and mix well. Shape into four patties. Grill over medium-hot heat for 4-5 minutes per side or until meat is no longer pink. Serve on buns; top with sauteed onions if desired. Store remaining seasoning blend in an airtight container. **Yield:** 4 servings.

Editor's Note: Purchased Cajun seasoning may be substituted for the homemade blend.

Grilling Gear

A WIDE metal spatula is ideal for turning burgers, steaks and fish fillets. Choose one with a long wooden handle and stainless steel blade.
A long-handled fork helps lift cooked meats, roasts and poultry from the grill. Avoid piercing the meat while it's cooking, though, or you may lose tasty juices.
An oven mitt provides protection from hot pans, utensils and the grill itself.

The Perfect Hamburger

(Pictured below)

Shirley Kidd, New London, Minnesota

Chili sauce and horseradish add zip to these hamburgers and make them a nice change from ordinary burgers. We think they're perfect and we make them often for family and friends, who agree.

    1 egg, lightly beaten
    2 tablespoons chili sauce
    1 teaspoon dried minced onion
    1 teaspoon prepared horseradish
    1 teaspoon Worcestershire sauce
  1/2 teaspoon salt
Pinch pepper
    1 pound lean ground beef
    4 hamburger buns, split
Optional toppings: sliced tomato, onion, pickles
  and condiments

In a large bowl, combine the first seven ingredients. Add beef and mix well. Shape into four 3/4-in.-thick patties. Grill, uncovered, over medium-hot heat for 5-6 minutes on each side or until meat is no longer

Sesame Steaks

(Pictured above)

Elaine Anderson, Aliquippa, Pennsylvania

There's enough flavor in these steaks to allow the side dish to be simple. So consider serving them with baked potatoes, rice pilaf or a plain vegetable and salad. The meal has always gone over big when I've fixed it for my husband and friends who help out with his latest home construction project.

  1/2 cup soy sauce
    2 tablespoons brown sugar
    2 tablespoons vegetable oil
    2 tablespoons sesame seeds
    2 teaspoons onion powder
    2 teaspoons lemon juice
  1/4 teaspoon ground ginger
    4 T-bone steaks (about 1 inch thick)

In a large resealable plastic bag or shallow glass container, combine the first seven ingredients; mix well. Add steaks and turn to coat. Cover and refrigerate for at least 4 hours. Drain and discard marinade.

Grill steaks, uncovered, over medium heat for 5-7 minutes on each side or until meat reaches desired doneness (for rare, a meat thermometer should read 140°; medium, 160°; well-done, 170°). **Yield:** 4 servings.

pink. Serve on buns with toppings of your choice. **Yield:** 4 servings.

Marinated Rib Eyes

(Pictured above)

Rosalie Usry, Flaxton, North Dakota

We have these tempting steaks weekly. Whenever I suggest a change in the recipe, my husband reminds me, "Don't fix it if it's not broken." If neighbors happen to drop by when I'm preparing steaks, I cut the meat into cubes and grill it on skewers with onions and mushrooms as appetizers.

　1/3　cup hot water
　　3　tablespoons finely chopped onion
　　2　tablespoons red wine vinegar *or* cider
　　　　vinegar
　　2　tablespoons olive *or* vegetable oil
　　2　tablespoons soy sauce
　　1　teaspoon beef bouillon granules
　　1　garlic clove, minced
　1/2　teaspoon paprika
　1/2　teaspoon coarsely ground pepper
　　2　beef rib eye steaks (about 1 inch thick and
　　　　12 ounces *each*)

In a bowl, combine the first nine ingredients. Remove 1/2 cup marinade and refrigerate. Pierce steaks several times on both sides with a fork; place in an 11-in. x 7-in. x 2-in. glass dish. Pour remaining marinade over steaks; turn to coat. Cover and refrigerate overnight. Remove steaks, discarding marinade.

Grill, uncovered, over medium-hot heat for 4-8 minutes on each side or until meat reaches desired donness (for rare, a meat thermometer should read 140°; medium, 160°; well-done, 170°). Warm reserved marinade; serve with steaks. **Yield:** 2 servings.

Tender Flank Steak

(Pictured on page 6)

Gayle Bucknam, Greenbank, Washington

This mildly marinated flank steak is my son's favorite. I usually slice it thinly and serve it with twice-baked potatoes and a green salad to round out the meal. Leftovers are great for French dip sandwiches.

 Uses less fat, sugar or salt. Includes Nutritional Analysis and Diabetic Exchanges.

　1/4　cup soy sauce
　　2　tablespoons water
　　3　garlic cloves, thinly sliced
　　1　tablespoon brown sugar
　　1　tablespoon vegetable oil
　1/2　teaspoon ground ginger
　1/2　teaspoon pepper
　　1　flank steak (1 pound)

In a large resealable plastic bag or shallow glass container, combine the first seven ingredients; mix well. Add steak and turn to coat. Cover and refrigerate for 8 hours or overnight, turning occasionally. Drain and discard marinade.

Grill, covered, over medium-hot heat for 6-8 minutes on each side or until meat reaches desired doneness (for rare, a meat thermometer should read 140°; medium, 160°; well-done, 170°). **Yield:** 4 servings.

Nutritional Analysis: One serving (prepared with reduced-sodium soy sauce) equals 209 calories, 326 mg sodium, 59 mg cholesterol, 3 gm carbohydrate, 24 gm protein, 11 gm fat, trace fiber. **Diabetic Exchange:** 3-1/2 lean meat.

Barbecued Chuck Roast

(Pictured below)

Ardis Gautier, Lamont, Oklahoma

Whether I serve this roast for church dinners, company or just family, it is always a hit. To go along with it, my family likes scalloped potatoes, tossed salad and pie. If there's ever any left over, it makes good sandwiches, too.

        1/3 cup cider vinegar
        1/4 cup ketchup
           2 tablespoons vegetable oil
           2 tablespoons soy sauce
           1 tablespoon Worcestershire sauce
           1 teaspoon garlic powder
           1 teaspoon prepared mustard
           1 teaspoon salt
        1/4 teaspoon pepper
           1 boneless chuck roast (2-1/2 to 3 pounds)
        1/2 cup applesauce

In a large resealable plastic bag or shallow glass container, combine the first nine ingredients; mix well. Add roast and turn to coat. Seal bag or cover container; refrigerate for at least 3 hours, turning occasionally. Remove roast. Pour marinade into a small saucepan; bring to a boil. Reduce heat; simmer for 15 minutes.

Meanwhile, grill roast, covered, over indirect heat for 20 minutes, turning occasionally. Add applesauce to marinade; brush over roast. Continue basting and turning the roast several times for 1 to 1-1/2 hours, or until meat reaches desired doneness (for rare, a meat thermometer should read 140°; medium, 160°; well-done, 170°). **Yield:** 6-8 servings.

Grilled Steak Pinwheels

(Pictured above)

Mary Hills, Scottsdale, Arizona

I've been serving this recipe to family and friends for over 20 years and very seldom do I have leftovers. We try to keep the house cool, so we grill out often. I get most of the herbs in this recipe from my son's garden.

           2 flank steaks (1 pound *each*), trimmed
        1/2 pound sliced bacon, cooked and crumbled
           1 cup finely chopped fresh mushrooms
           1 cup finely chopped green onions
        1/4 cup finely chopped fresh basil *or* 4
             teaspoons dried basil
           2 tablespoons minced fresh chives

Pound flank steaks on each side. Combine bacon, mushrooms, onions, basil and chives; spread evenly over steaks. Roll the meat up and secure with skewers or wooden picks. Cut each roll into 1/2- to 3/4-in. slices and secure with a wooden pick or skewer.

Grill over hot heat for 4-6 minutes per side or until meat reaches desired doneness. Remove picks before serving. **Yield:** 6-8 servings.

Sirloin Caesar Salad

(Pictured below)

Carol Sinclair, St. Elmo, Illinois

A tangy sauce that combines bottled salad dressing, lemon juice and Dijon mustard flavors this filling main-dish salad. You save on cleanup time because both the steak and bread are cooked on the grill.

 Uses less fat, sugar or salt. Includes Nutritional Analysis and Diabetic Exchanges.

  1 boneless top sirloin steak (1 pound)
  1 cup Caesar salad dressing
1/4 cup Dijon mustard
1/4 cup lemon juice
  6 slices French bread (1 inch thick)
 12 cups torn romaine
  1 medium tomato, chopped

Place steak in a large resealable plastic bag or shallow glass container. In a bowl, combine salad dressing, mustard and lemon juice; set aside 3/4 cup. Pour remaining dressing mixture over steak. Seal or cover and refrigerate for 1 hour, turning occasionally.

Brush both sides of bread with 1/4 cup of the reserved dressing mixture. Grill bread, uncovered, over medium heat for 1-2 minutes on each side or until lightly toasted. Wrap in foil and set aside.

Drain steak, discarding marinade. Grill, covered, for 5-8 minutes on each side or until meat reaches desired doneness (for rare, a meat thermometer should read 140°; medium, 160°; well-done, 170°). Place romaine and tomato on serving platter. Slice steak diagonally; arrange over salad. Serve with the bread and remaining dressing. **Yield:** 6 servings.

Nutritional Analysis: One serving (prepared with fat-free dressing) equals 214 calories, 586 mg sodium, 50 mg cholesterol, 18 gm carbohydrate, 22 gm protein, 6 gm fat. **Diabetic Exchanges:** 2 lean meat, 1 starch, 1 vegetable.

Citrus Sirloin Steak

Carol Towey, Pasadena, California

The mild citrus flavor of this marinade offers a nice change of pace from usual steak seasonings. It's easy to prepare the steak the night before, then throw it on the grill before dinner.

  2 medium unpeeled lemons, quartered
  1 medium unpeeled orange, quartered
1/2 cup vegetable oil
  1 garlic clove, minced
  1 boneless sirloin steak (about 2-1/2 pounds and 1-3/4 inches thick)

In a skillet, cook the lemon and orange wedges in oil over medium heat for 10-15 minutes, stirring often. Add garlic; cook and stir 1-2 minutes longer.

Place steak in a shallow glass baking dish; pierce meat every inch with a fork. Pour citrus mixture over meat; turn to coat. Cover and refrigerate overnight, turning three or four times.

Drain and discard marinade. Grill steak, covered, over medium-hot heat for 9-10 minutes on each side or until meat reaches desired doneness (for rare, a meat thermometer should read 140°; medium, 160°; well-done, 170°). **Yield:** 6-8 servings.

Basil-Stuffed Steak

(Pictured above)

Linda Gronewaller, Hutchinson, Kansas

This is a recipe I developed. We love beef, and grilling is an easy way to add variety to our meals. My mom and grandma taught me how to cook when I was young. I've entered several cooking competitions and have won some awards.

    1 boneless sirloin steak (2 to 2-1/2 pounds
        and about 1-1/2 inches thick)
  1/2 teaspoon salt
  1/4 teaspoon pepper
  1/4 teaspoon dried parsley flakes
1-1/2 cups lightly packed fresh basil
  1/4 cup finely chopped onion
    4 garlic cloves, minced
1-1/2 teaspoons minced fresh rosemary *or* 1/2
        teaspoon dried rosemary, crushed
  1/8 teaspoon minced fresh thyme *or* pinch
        dried thyme
    1 teaspoon olive *or* vegetable oil

With a sharp knife, make five lengthwise cuts three-fourths of the way through the steak. Combine salt, pepper and parsley; rub over steak. Coarsely chop the basil; add onion, garlic, rosemary and thyme.

Stuff into pockets in steak; using heavy-duty string, tie the steak at 2-in. intervals, closing the pockets. Drizzle with oil. Grill, covered, over indirect medium heat for 35-45 minutes or until the meat reach-

es desired doneness (for rare, a meat thermometer should read 140°; medium, 160°; well-done, 170°). Cover and let stand for 5-10 minutes. Remove string before slicing. **Yield:** 6-8 servings.

Skewered Ginger Beef

Jean Gaines, Russellville, Kentucky

I marinate and skewer several servings of this dish, freezing extras for future events. Not only do these tender slices of beef make a quick and easy dinner, but they make impressive appetizers, too.

    1 cup sugar
    1 cup soy sauce
  1/2 cup vegetable oil
    1 bunch green onions, sliced
    6 garlic cloves, minced
  1/4 cup sesame seeds, toasted
  3/4 teaspoon ground ginger *or* 2 teaspoons
        grated fresh gingerroot
    2 teaspoons pepper
    2 pounds beef sirloin steak, cut into
        1/4-inch strips

In a large resealable plastic bag, combine the first eight ingredients; add steak. Seal bag and turn to coat; refrigerate for 8 hours or overnight. Drain and discard marinade.

Thread steak onto metal or soaked wooden skewers. Grill, covered, over indirect medium heat for 15 minutes or until meat reaches desired doneness, turning occasionally. **Yield:** 8 servings.

T-Bones with Onions

(Pictured at right)

Sheree Quate, Cave Junction, Oregon

T-bone steaks get a dressy treatment when topped with tasty onion slices flavored with honey and ground mustard. I found this recipe on a bag of charcoal more than 10 years ago and have been making it ever since. It's terrific with green beans or corn.

3 large onions, cut into 1/4-inch-thick slices
2 tablespoons honey
1/2 teaspoon salt
1/2 teaspoon pepper
1/2 teaspoon ground mustard
1/2 teaspoon paprika
4 T-bone steaks

Place onions in the center of a piece of heavy-duty foil (about 20 in. x 18 in.). Drizzle with honey; sprinkle with salt, pepper, mustard and paprika. Fold foil over onions; seal tightly. Grill, uncovered, over medium-hot heat for 20-25 minutes or until tender, turning once.

Grill the steaks, uncovered, over medium-hot heat for 12-26 minutes, turning once, or until meat reaches desired doneness (for rare, a meat thermometer should read 140°; medium, 160°; well-done, 170°). Serve with onions. **Yield:** 4 servings.

Peppered Steaks with Salsa

(Pictured above right)

Robin Hyde, Lincoln, Nebraska

We grill all year, and beef is so good cooked outdoors. The simple marinade makes the steaks very juicy. We enjoy them with the refreshing salsa and tortillas.

1/2 cup red wine vinegar *or* cider vinegar
2 tablespoons lime juice

2 tablespoons olive *or* vegetable oil
2 teaspoons chili powder
1 garlic clove, minced
1 to 2 teaspoons crushed red pepper flakes
1 teaspoon salt
1/2 teaspoon pepper
4 boneless chuck eye steaks (about 8 ounces *each*)
SALSA:
1 large tomato, seeded and chopped
1 medium ripe avocado, chopped
2 green onions, thinly sliced
1 tablespoon lime juice
1 tablespoon minced fresh cilantro *or* parsley
1 garlic clove, minced
1/4 to 1/2 teaspoon salt
1/4 teaspoon pepper

In a large resealable plastic bag or shallow glass container, combine the first eight ingredients; mix well. Remove 1/4 cup for basting; refrigerate. Add steaks to the remaining marinade; turn to coat. Cover and refrigerate 8 hours or overnight. Meanwhile, combine salsa ingredients; cover and chill.

Drain steaks, discarding marinade. Grill, covered, over medium heat for 7-8 minutes on each side, basting with reserved marinade, or until meat reaches desired doneness (for rare, a meat thermometer should read 140°; medium, 160°; well-done, 170°). Serve with salsa. **Yield:** 4 servings.

Grilled Pizza Bread

(Pictured at right)

Edna Hoffman, Hebron, Indiana

These fun French bread pizzas are great picnic fare for both kids and adults. Tasty on the grill, they can just as easily be baked in the oven.

    1 pound ground beef
1/2 cup chopped onion
    1 can (8 ounces) tomato sauce
1/2 teaspoon salt
1/2 teaspoon dried oregano
    1 loaf (1 pound) French bread
    1 cup (4 ounces) shredded mozzarella cheese
    1 can (2-1/4 ounces) sliced ripe olives, drained
Sliced pepperoni, optional

In a skillet over medium heat, cook beef and onion until meat is browned and onion is tender; drain. Stir in the tomato sauce, salt and oregano; simmer for 5-10 minutes.

Cut bread in half lengthwise and then widthwise. Spread meat mixture on cut side of bread; sprinkle with cheese, olives and pepperoni if desired. Loosely wrap bread individually in pieces of heavy-duty foil (about 24 in. x 18 in.); seal. Grill, covered, over medium heat for 15-20 minutes or until heated through. **Yield:** 4-6 servings.

Steak with Citrus Salsa

(Pictured below left)

Kathleen Smith, Pittsburgh, Pennsylvania

A lime juice marinade really perks up grilled steaks, and the snappy, light citrus salsa is a super change from the usual heavy steak sauce. My family loves steak served this way.

1/2 cup soy sauce
1/4 cup chopped green onions
    3 tablespoons lime juice
    2 tablespoons brown sugar
1/8 teaspoon hot pepper sauce
    1 garlic clove, minced
1-1/2 pounds boneless sirloin steak (about 1 inch thick)
SALSA:
    2 navel oranges, peeled, sectioned and chopped
1/4 cup chopped green onions
    2 tablespoons orange juice
    2 tablespoons red wine vinegar *or* cider vinegar
    2 tablespoons chopped lemon
    1 tablespoon chopped lime
    1 tablespoon sugar
    1 tablespoon minced fresh cilantro *or* parsley
    1 teaspoon minced jalapeno pepper*
1/2 teaspoon grated lemon peel
1/2 teaspoon grated lime peel
1/8 teaspoon salt

In a large resealable plastic bag, combine the first six ingredients; add beef. Seal and refrigerate for 2 hours or overnight, turning occasionally. Drain and discard

marinade. Grill steak, uncovered, over medium heat for 4-6 minutes on each side or until meat reaches desired doneness (for rare, a meat thermometer should read 140°; medium, 160°; well-done, 170°).

Combine salsa ingredients in a bowl. Cut steak across the grain into thin slices. Serve with salsa. **Yield:** 4-6 servings.

*Editor's Note: When cutting or seeding hot peppers, use rubber or plastic gloves to protect your hands. Avoid touching your face.

Pasta Salad with Steak

(Pictured below)

Julie DeRuwe, Oakville, Washington

While there are quite a few ingredients in this recipe, it doesn't take too long to make—and cleanup afterward's a snap.

3/4 cup olive *or* vegetable oil
2 tablespoons lemon juice
2 teaspoons dried oregano
1 tablespoon Dijon mustard

2 teaspoons red wine vinegar *or* cider vinegar
1 teaspoon sugar
1/2 teaspoon salt
1/2 teaspoon pepper
3 cups cooked small shell pasta
1 sirloin steak (1 pound)
RUB:
1 tablespoon olive *or* vegetable oil
3 garlic cloves, minced
2 teaspoons dried oregano
2 teaspoons pepper
1 teaspoon sugar
SALAD:
2/3 cup diced cucumber
1/2 cup crumbled blue *or* feta cheese
1/4 cup sliced ripe olives
1/4 cup chopped red onion
1/4 cup minced fresh parsley
1 jar (2 ounces) diced pimientos, drained
Iceberg *or* romaine lettuce

In a bowl, combine the first eight ingredients; set half of the dressing aside. Place pasta in another bowl; add remaining dressing. Toss to coat; cover and refrigerate.

Pierce steak with a fork. Combine rub ingredients; rub over steak. Cover and refrigerate for at least 15 minutes. Grill steak, uncovered, over medium heat for 9-10 minutes on each side or until meat reaches desired doneness (for rare, a meat thermometer should read 140°; medium, 160°; well-done, 170°). Let stand for 10 minutes.

Meanwhile, add the cucumber, cheese, olives, onion, parsley and pimientos to the pasta; mix well. Spoon onto a lettuce-lined platter. Slice the steak and arrange over salad. Serve with reserved dressing. **Yield:** 4 servings.

Marinating Meat

MARINADES can be used to add flavor to meat and vegetables or tenderize less-tender cuts of meat. Always marinate in the refrigerator in a glass container or resealable plastic bag.

In general, do not reuse marinades. If a marinade is to be used as a basting or dipping sauce, reserve a portion before adding the uncooked foods. Or bring the used marinade to a rolling boil.

Beef and Pepper Kabobs

(Pictured above)

Janet Wood, Windham, New Hampshire

I've traveled to many different countries and am always on the lookout for cookbooks. I adapted this recipe from a Turkish cookbook and it brings rave reviews whenever I serve it.

    3 tablespoons lemon juice
    2 tablespoons vegetable oil
    1 large onion, finely chopped
1-1/2 teaspoons dried thyme
    1/2 teaspoon salt
    1/4 teaspoon pepper
    2 pounds sirloin, cut into 1-inch cubes
    1 *each* green, yellow, orange and red
      peppers

In a resealable plastic bag or shallow glass container, combine lemon juice, oil, onion, thyme, salt and pepper. Add meat; turn to coat. Seal bag or cover container; refrigerate 6 hours or overnight. Drain and discard marinade.

    Cut peppers into 1-in. squares and thread onto metal or soaked wooden skewers alternately with meat. Grill over hot heat, turning often, for 12-15 minutes or until the meat reaches desired doneness. **Yield:** 6-8 servings.

Hawaiian Honey Burgers

(Pictured below)

Sheryl Creech, Lancaster, California

These burgers were a favorite when I was growing up. I now use them as a way to "fancy up" a barbecue without a lot of extra preparation. They keep me out of a hot kitchen yet let me serve a nice meal. Fresh fruit and corn on the cob are wonderful accompaniments.

    1/2 cup honey
    1/4 teaspoon ground cinnamon
    1/4 teaspoon paprika
    1/4 teaspoon curry powder
    1/8 teaspoon ground ginger
    1/8 teaspoon ground nutmeg
    2 pounds ground beef
    1/4 cup soy sauce
    1 can (23 ounces) sliced pineapple, drained
    8 hamburger buns, split and toasted
Lettuce leaves, optional

In a bowl, combine the first six ingredients; add beef and mix well. Shape into eight 3/4-in.-thick patties. Grill the burgers, uncovered, over medium-hot heat for 3 minutes on each side. Brush with soy sauce. Continue grilling for 4-6 minutes or meat is no longer pink, basting and turning several times.

    During the last 4 minutes, grill the pineapple slices until browned, turning once. Serve burgers and pineapple on buns with lettuce if desired. **Yield:** 8 servings.

horseradish and garlic. Cook and stir over medium heat until sugar is dissolved, about 3 minutes. Pour mixture into a disposable aluminum pan; set aside.

In a large skillet, brown brisket on both sides in remaining oil. Place brisket in pan; turn to coat with sauce. Cover pan tightly with foil.

Grill, covered, over indirect medium heat for 1 hour. Add 10 briquettes to coals. Cover and cook about 1-1/4 hours longer, adding more briquettes if needed, or until meat reaches desired doneness (for rare, a meat thermometer should read 140°; medium, 160°; well-done, 170°). Slice beef; serve with pan drippings. **Yield:** 6-8 servings.

*Editor's Note: This is a fresh brisket, not corned beef.

Marinated Sirloin Steak

Karen Mattern, Spokane, Washington

I once knew a nun who cooked the best marinated steaks. I found this recipe in my quest to fix steaks that were as good as hers. This delicious, versatile meat makes a special holiday main dish or a super camping supper.

    2 to 2-1/2 pounds sirloin steak (about 1
       inch thick)
1-1/2 cups water
  3/4 cup soy sauce
  1/4 cup Worcestershire sauce
    1 medium onion, chopped
    2 tablespoons white wine vinegar *or* cider
       vinegar
    2 tablespoons lemon juice
    2 tablespoons Dijon mustard
    2 garlic cloves, minced
    2 teaspoons dried parsley flakes
    1 teaspoon dried thyme
    1 teaspoon Italian seasoning
    1 teaspoon pepper

Place the steak in a shallow glass container or large heavy-duty resealable plastic bag. Combine all of the remaining ingredients; pour over the meat. Cover or seal and refrigerate overnight. Drain and discard the marinade.

Grill steak, uncovered, over medium heat until meat reaches desired doneness, about 6-7 minutes per side for rare, 8-10 minutes per side for medium or 11-13 minutes for well-done. **Yield:** 6 servings.

Barbecued Beef Brisket

(Pictured above)

Bettye Miller, Blanchard, Oklahoma

A guest at the RV park and marina my husband and I used to run gave me this flavorful brisket recipe. It's become the star of countless meal gatherings, from potlucks to holiday dinners. My husband, Ed, and our five grown children look forward to it as much as our Christmas turkey.

1/2 cup packed brown sugar
1/2 cup ketchup
1/4 cup water
1/4 cup cider vinegar
  6 tablespoons vegetable oil, *divided*
  3 tablespoons dark corn syrup
  2 tablespoons prepared mustard
  1 tablespoon prepared horseradish
  1 garlic clove, minced
  1 fresh beef brisket (2 to 2-1/2 pounds)*,
     trimmed

In a saucepan, combine the brown sugar, ketchup, water, vinegar, 4 tablespoons oil, corn syrup, mustard,

Grilled Cheeseburger Pizza

(Pictured below)

Tanya Gutierro, Beacon Falls, Connecticut

I combined our daughter's two favorite foods—pizza and grilled cheeseburgers—to create this main dish. It's very simple to make, and she and her friends love it. If you don't like the toppings, replace them with whatever you prefer.

 3/4 pound ground beef
 1 cup ketchup
 2 tablespoons prepared mustard
 1 prebaked Italian bread shell crust
 (14 ounces)
 1 cup shredded lettuce
 1 medium tomato, thinly sliced
 1/8 teaspoon salt
 1/8 teaspoon pepper
 1 small sweet onion, thinly sliced
 1/2 cup dill pickle slices
 1 cup (4 ounces) shredded cheddar cheese
 1 cup (4 ounces) shredded mozzarella cheese

Shape beef into three 1/2-in.-thick patties. Grill, covered, over medium-hot heat for 5 minutes on each side or until meat is no longer pink. Meanwhile, combine ketchup and mustard; spread over the crust to within 1 in. of edge. Sprinkle with lettuce; top with tomato. Sprinkle with salt and pepper. When beef patties are cooked, cut into 1/2-in. pieces; arrange over tomato

slices. Top with onion, pickles and cheeses.

Place pizza on a 16-in. square piece of heavy-duty foil; transfer to grill. Grill, covered, over indirect medium heat for 12-15 minutes or until cheese is melted and crust is lightly browned. Remove from the grill. Let stand for 5-10 minutes before slicing. **Yield:** 4-6 servings.

Sirloin Squash Shish Kabobs

(Pictured above)

Ronda Karbo, Russell, Minnesota

When our grill comes out in the spring, this is the first recipe my family asks me to make. You can also use this marinade on six pork chops or a large piece of round steak cut into serving-size pieces.

 1 cup packed brown sugar
 1 cup soy sauce
 1 teaspoon *each* garlic powder, ground
 mustard and ground ginger
 1 pound boneless beef sirloin steak, cut into
 1-inch pieces
 1 medium zucchini, cut into 1/4-inch slices
 1 medium yellow summer squash, cut into
 1/4-inch slices
 1 medium sweet red pepper, cut into 1-inch
 pieces
 1 medium red onion, cut into eight wedges,
 optional

In a bowl, combine the brown sugar, soy sauce, garlic powder, mustard and ginger. Place beef in a large resealable plastic bag; add 1 cup marinade. Seal bag and toss to coat. Place zucchini, yellow squash, red pepper and onion if desired in another resealable bag; add remaining marinade and toss to coat. Refrigerate beef and vegetables for at least 4 hours, turning occasionally.

Drain and discard marinade. On eight metal or soaked wooden skewers, alternately thread beef and vegetables. Grill, covered, over medium-hot heat for 10 minutes or until meat reaches desired doneness, turning occasionally. **Yield:** 4 servings.

Giant Stuffed Picnic Burger

(Pictured below)

Helen Hudson, Brockville, Ontario

Guests will be delighted when they sink their teeth into juicy wedges of this full-flavored burger. The moist filling is chock-full of mushrooms, onion and parsley. It's a great alternative to regular burgers.

**2 pounds ground beef
1 teaspoon salt**

1 teaspoon Worcestershire sauce
3/4 cup crushed seasoned stuffing mix
1 can (4 ounces) mushroom stems and pieces, drained
1/4 cup beef broth
1/4 cup minced fresh parsley
1/4 cup sliced green onions
1 egg, beaten
1 tablespoon butter *or* margarine, melted
1 teaspoon lemon juice

Combine beef, salt and Worcestershire sauce. Divide in half; pat each half into an 8-in. circle on waxed paper. Combine the remaining ingredients; spoon over one patty to within 1 in. of the edge. Top with second patty; press edges to seal.

Grill, covered, over medium heat for 12-13 minutes on each side or until the juices run clear. Cut into wedges. **Yield:** 6 servings.

Editor's Note: Stuffed burger may be placed directly on the grill or in a well-greased wire grill basket.

Tacos on a Stick

Dixie Terry, Goreville, Illinois

Teens like assembling these creative kabobs almost as much as they like devouring them. The whole family is sure to love the sensational Southwestern flavor of this twist on beef shish kabobs.

1 envelope taco seasoning
1 cup tomato juice
2 to 4 tablespoons vegetable oil
2 pounds boneless beef top sirloin, cut into 1-inch cubes
1 medium green pepper, cut into chunks
1 medium sweet red pepper, cut into chunks
1 large onion, cut into wedges
16 cherry tomatoes

In a large resealable plastic bag, combine the taco seasoning, tomato juice and oil; mix well. Remove 1/2 cup for basting; refrigerate. Add beef to the bag; seal and turn to coat. Refrigerate for at least 5 hours.

Drain and discard marinade from beef. On metal or soaked wooden skewers, alternately thread beef, peppers, onion and tomatoes. Grill, uncovered, over medium heat for 3 minutes on each side. Baste with reserved marinade. Continue turning and basting for 8-10 minutes or until meat reaches desired doneness. **Yield:** 6 servings.

Chili Flank Steak

(Pictured above)

Karma Henry, Glasgow, Kentucky

I started making this recipe when we moved from Idaho to Kentucky. It gets so hot here that we use our outdoor grill as often as possible to keep the kitchen cool. My husband loves this juicy steak and its tasty sauce. I like that I can have it ready to marinate in no time.

2/3 cup packed brown sugar
2/3 cup V8 juice
2/3 cup soy sauce
1/2 cup olive *or* vegetable oil
4 garlic cloves, chopped
2 tablespoons chili powder
1/4 teaspoon ground cumin
1 beef flank steak (about 1-1/2 pounds)

In a large bowl, combine the first seven ingredients; mix well. Pour half of the marinade into a large resealable bag; add the steak. Seal bag and turn to coat; refrigerate for 8 hours or overnight, turning occasionally. Cover and refrigerate the remaining marinade.

Drain and discard marinade from steak. Grill steak, covered, over medium-hot heat for 6-10 minutes on each side or until meat reaches desired doneness (for rare, a meat thermometer should read 140°; medium, 160°; well-done, 170°). Serve with reserved marinade. **Yield:** 4-6 servings.

Onion-Smothered Sirloins

(Pictured below)

Tina Michalicka, Hudson, Florida

Friends and family love these savory steaks and sweet onions. The dinner is simple to prepare and the flavor is fantastic. I usually serve it with corn and baked potatoes cooked on the grill as well. For spicier steaks, increase the pepper flakes and cumin.

1 teaspoon garlic powder
3/4 teaspoon salt, *divided*
1/2 teaspoon ground cumin
1/2 teaspoon dried oregano
1/4 teaspoon crushed red pepper flakes
4 boneless beef sirloin steaks (about 8 ounces *each* and 1 inch thick)
2 large sweet onions, cut into 1/2-inch slices and separated into rings
1/4 cup olive *or* vegetable oil
1/4 teaspoon pepper
1 medium lime, cut into quarters

In a bowl, combine the garlic powder, 1/2 teaspoon salt, cumin, oregano and pepper flakes. Rub over the steaks; set aside. Place onions in a disposable foil pan; add oil and toss to coat. Grill, covered, over medium heat for 30-40 minutes or until golden brown, stirring occasionally. Season onions with pepper, remaining salt and a squeeze of lime.

Grill steaks, uncovered, over medium heat for 7-10 minutes on each side or until meat reaches desired doneness (for rare, a meat thermometer should read

140°; medium, 160°; well-done, 170°). Squeeze remaining lime over the steaks; top with onions. **Yield:** 4 servings.

Spinach Steak Pinwheels

(Pictured above)

Helen Vail, Glenside, Pennsylvania

Bacon and spinach bring plenty of flavor to these sirloin steak spirals. It's an easy dish to make and great to grill at a backyard cookout. I get lots of compliments on it, no matter how many times I serve it.

1-1/2 pounds boneless beef sirloin steak
    8 bacon strips, cooked and drained
    1 package (10 ounces) frozen chopped spinach, thawed and squeezed dry
1/4 cup grated Parmesan cheese
1/2 teaspoon salt
1/8 teaspoon cayenne pepper

Make diagonal cuts in steak at 1-in. intervals to within 1/2 in. of bottom of meat. Repeat cuts in opposite direction. Pound to 1/2-in. thickness. Place bacon down the center of the meat. In a bowl, combine the spinach, Parmesan cheese, salt and cayenne; spoon over bacon. Roll up and secure with toothpicks. Cut into six slices.

Grill, uncovered, over medium heat for 6 minutes on each side or until meat reaches desired doneness (for rare, a meat thermometer should read 140°; medium, 160°; well-done, 170°). Discard toothpicks. **Yield:** 6 servings.

Grilled Rib Eye Steaks

Tim Hanchon, Muncie, Indiana

In summer, I love to marinate these steaks overnight, then grill them for family and friends the next day. When the weather is not as nice, they can be cooked under the broiler in the oven.

1/2 cup soy sauce
1/2 cup sliced green onions
1/4 cup packed brown sugar
    2 garlic cloves, minced
1/4 teaspoon ground ginger
1/4 teaspoon pepper
2-1/2 pounds beef rib eye steaks

In a large resealable plastic bag, combine the soy sauce, onions, brown sugar, garlic, ginger and pepper. Add the steaks. Seal bag and turn to coat; refrigerate for 8 hours or overnight.

Drain and discard marinade. Grill steaks, uncovered, over medium-hot heat for 8-10 minutes or until the meat reaches desired doneness (for rare, a meat thermometer should read 140°; medium, 160°; well-done, 170°). **Yield:** 8-10 servings.

Buying Beef

WHEN purchasing beef, look for brightly colored, red to deep-red cuts. Marbeling—flecks or streaks of fat in the meat—should be moderate.

The most tender beef cuts (rib, short loin and sirloin) come from the animal's most lightly exercised muscles, namely along the upper back. Heavily used muscles produce less tender cuts, such as chuck (near the animal's front end) and round (from the rear).

Choose packages that are cool to the touch, have little or no excess liquid and have no punctures.

Chicken and Turkey

Grilled Turkey Tenderloin (p. 47)

Chapter 2

In a bowl, combine the first eight ingredients; mix well. Pour half of marinade into a large resealable plastic bag; add meat and turn to coat. Pour remaining marinade into another large resealable plastic bag. Add vegetables and turn to coat. Seal and refrigerate for 8 hours or overnight, turning occasionally.

Drain meat, discarding marinade. Drain vegetables, reserving marinade for basting. On metal or soaked wooden skewers, alternate meat, vegetables and lime wedges. Grill, uncovered, over medium heat for 4-5 minutes on each side. Baste with reserved marinade. Continue turning and basting for 10-12 minutes or until meat juices run clear and vegetables are tender. **Yield:** 8 servings.

*Editor's Note: When cutting or seeding hot peppers, use rubber or plastic gloves to protect your hands. Avoid touching your face.

Turkey Lime Kabobs

(Pictured above)

Shelly Johnston, Rochester, Minnesota

My husband loves to grill these deliciously different turkey kabobs, and everyone gets a kick out of the zingy taste from the limes and jalapenos. Its tongue-tingling combination of flavors makes this one company dish that always draws compliments.

        3 cans (6 ounces *each*) orange juice
          concentrate, thawed
  1-1/4 cups lime juice
        1 cup honey
        4 to 5 jalapeno peppers, seeded and
          chopped*
      10 garlic cloves, minced
        3 tablespoons ground cumin
        2 tablespoons grated lime peel
        1 teaspoon salt
        2 pounds boneless turkey, chicken *or* pork,
          cut into 1-1/4-inch cubes
        4 medium sweet red *or* green peppers, cut
          into 1-inch pieces
        1 large red onion, cut into 1-inch pieces
        3 small zucchini, cut into 3/4-inch slices
        8 ounces fresh mushrooms
        3 medium limes, cut into wedges

Grilled Chicken with Peach Sauce

(Pictured below)

Beverly Minton, Milan, Michigan

I've been cooking since I was a young girl growing up on a farm in Indiana. This recipe was adapted from a pie filling. I've served it many times to family and friends.

1 cup sugar
2 tablespoons cornstarch
1 cup water
2 tablespoons peach gelatin powder
1 medium fresh peach, peeled and finely chopped
4 boneless skinless chicken breast halves (1-1/4 pounds)

In a saucepan, combine sugar, cornstarch and water until smooth. Bring to a boil over medium heat; cook and stir for 2 minutes. Remove from heat. Stir in the gelatin and peach; mix well. Set aside 1 cup.

Grill chicken, uncovered, over medium heat for 3 minutes on each side. Baste with some of the remaining peach sauce. Continue grilling for 6-8 minutes or until meat juices run clear, basting and turning several times. Serve with the reserved peach sauce. **Yield:** 4 servings.

Summertime Chicken Tacos

(Pictured above right)

Susan Scott, Asheville, North Carolina

Try these tempting tacos when you're looking for a change of pace from regular tacos. A mild zing from the lime juice in the marinade for the chicken comes through after grilling.

 Uses less fat, sugar or salt. Includes Nutritional Analysis and Diabetic Exchanges.

1/3 cup olive *or* vegetable oil
1/4 cup lime juice
4 garlic cloves, minced
1 tablespoon minced fresh parsley *or* 1 teaspoon dried parsley flakes
1 teaspoon ground cumin
1 teaspoon dried oregano
1/2 teaspoon salt, optional
1/4 teaspoon pepper
4 boneless skinless chicken breast halves (1-1/4 pounds)
6 flour tortillas (8 inches) *or* taco shells, warmed
Toppings of your choice

In a large resealable plastic bag or shallow glass container, combine the first eight ingredients. Add chicken and turn to coat. Seal or cover and refrigerate 8 hours or overnight, turning occasionally. Drain and discard marinade.

Grill chicken, uncovered, over medium heat for 5-7 minutes on each side or until juices run clear. Cut into thin strips; serve in tortillas or taco shells with desired toppings. **Yield:** 6 servings.

Nutritional Analysis: One serving (prepared with flour tortillas and without salt; calculated without toppings) equals 338 calories, 289 mg sodium, 63 mg cholesterol, 28 gm carbohydrate, 27 gm protein, 12 gm fat. **Diabetic Exchanges:** 3 lean meat, 2 starch, 1/2 fat.

Poultry Pointers

BACTERIA flourish in poultry at temperatures between 40° and 140°, so don't let it sit out at room temperature too long before cooking.

Bacteria on raw poultry can contaminate other food it comes in contact with, so it's vital you always use hot soapy water to thoroughly wash your hands, cutting board and any utensils used in preparation of poultry.

Never let raw juices come in contact with cooked poultry.

Garden Turkey Burgers

(Pictured below)

Sandy Kitzmiller, Unityville, Pennsylvania

These moist burgers get plenty of color and flavor from onion, zucchini and red pepper. I often make the mixture ahead of time and put it in the refrigerator. Later, after helping my husband with farm chores, I can put the burgers on the grill while whipping up a salad.

 Uses less fat, sugar or salt. Includes Nutritional Analysis and Diabetic Exchanges.

  1 cup old-fashioned oats
3/4 cup chopped onion
3/4 cup finely chopped sweet red *or* green
      pepper
1/2 cup shredded zucchini
1/4 cup ketchup
  2 garlic cloves, minced
1/4 teaspoon salt, optional
  1 pound ground turkey
  6 whole wheat hamburger buns, split and
      toasted

Coat grill rack with nonstick cooking spray before starting the grill. In a bowl, combine the first seven ingredients. Add turkey and mix well. Shape into six 1/2-in.-thick patties.

Grill, covered, over indirect medium heat for 6 minutes on each side or until a meat thermometer reads 165°. Serve on buns. **Yield:** 6 burgers.

Nutritional Analysis: One serving (prepared with ground turkey breast and without salt; calculated without the bun) equals 156 calories, 174 mg sodium, 37 mg cholesterol, 15 gm carbohydrate, 21 gm protein, 2 gm fat. **Diabetic Exchanges:** 2 very lean meat, 1 starch.

Lemon-Lime Chicken

(Pictured above)

Dana Fulton, Stone Mountain, Georgia

I've served this main dish numerous times for dinner guests and have received many compliments. In fact, every time I make it for my husband, he'll comment, "This is the best chicken I've ever had."

  6 boneless skinless chicken breast halves
      (1-1/2 pounds)
1/2 cup packed brown sugar
1/4 cup cider vinegar
  3 tablespoons *each* lemon juice and lime juice
  3 tablespoons Dijon mustard
3/4 teaspoon garlic powder
1/4 teaspoon pepper
1/2 teaspoon salt

Place chicken in a shallow glass dish. Combine remaining ingredients; pour over chicken. Cover and refrigerate at least 4 hours or overnight. Drain, discarding marinade. Grill chicken over medium-hot heat, turning once, until juices run clear, about 15-18 minutes. **Yield:** 4-6 servings.

Grilled Chicken Pasta Salad

(Pictured below right)

Lori Thon, Basin, Wyoming

During the summer, my family often requests this recipe. Simply add garlic bread for a great meal. It's wonderful, too, for a picnic or any gathering.

1-1/2 cups Italian salad dressing
  1/2 cup cider vinegar
  1/3 cup honey
    2 teaspoons dried oregano
    1 teaspoon dried basil
  1/2 teaspoon pepper
    6 boneless skinless chicken breast halves
      (1-1/2 pounds)
    1 package (12 ounces) fettuccine
1-1/2 cups broccoli florets
    3 medium carrots, thinly sliced
    2 celery ribs, thinly sliced
    1 cup chopped green pepper
    2 cans (2-1/4 ounces *each*) sliced ripe olives,
      drained
DRESSING:
1-1/2 cups Italian salad dressing
    1 teaspoon garlic salt
    1 teaspoon dried oregano
    1 teaspoon Italian seasoning

In a large resealable plastic bag or shallow glass container, combine the first six ingredients. Cut each chicken breast into four strips; add to dressing mixture. Seal or cover and refrigerate for 2-3 hours. Drain and discard marinade. Grill chicken, uncovered, over medium heat for 4-5 minutes on each side or until juices run clear.

Meanwhile, cook fettuccine according to package directions; drain and cool. Cut chicken into bite-size pieces; set aside. In a large bowl, combine vegetables, olives and fettuccine. Combine dressing ingredients in a jar with a tight-fitting lid; shake well. Pour over salad and toss to coat. Top with chicken. **Yield:** 6 servings.

Maple Mustard Chicken

Lynda Ebel, Medicine Hat, Alberta

For make-ahead convenience, marinate these chicken breasts overnight. Their sweet and mustardy flavor goes well with baked potatoes and a tossed salad. They'd make delightful chicken sandwiches, too.

  1/2 cup maple syrup
    3 tablespoons red wine vinegar *or* cider vinegar
    2 tablespoons Dijon mustard
    1 tablespoon vegetable oil
    2 garlic cloves, minced
  3/4 to 1 teaspoon pepper
    6 boneless skinless chicken breast halves
      (1-1/2 pounds)

In a bowl, combine the first six ingredients; mix well. Reserve 1/4 cup for basting; cover and refrigerate. Pour remaining marinade into a large resealable plastic bag or shallow glass container; add chicken and turn to coat. Seal or cover; refrigerate for 4-8 hours, turning occasionally. Drain and discard marinade.

Grill, uncovered, over medium heat for 3 minutes on each side. Grill 6-8 minutes longer or until juices run clear, basting with the reserved marinade and turning occasionally. **Yield:** 6 servings.

Grilled Orange Chicken Strips

(Pictured above)

Marion Lowery, Medford, Oregon

These savory marinated chicken strips are great for a picnic or backyard barbecue. I grill them right along with sausages and hot dogs. Skewering the chicken makes it easy to handle, but you can put the strips directly on the grill if you prefer.

✓ Uses less fat, sugar or salt. Includes Nutritional Analysis and Diabetic Exchanges.

  2 tablespoons chopped fresh orange
    segments
1/4 cup orange juice
1/4 cup olive *or* vegetable oil
  2 teaspoons lime juice
  3 garlic cloves, minced
  1 teaspoon dried thyme
  1 teaspoon dried oregano
  1 teaspoon ground cumin
1/2 teaspoon salt, optional
  1 pound boneless skinless chicken breasts,
    cut into 1/4-inch strips

Combine the first nine ingredients in a resealable plastic bag or shallow glass container; add chicken and turn to coat. Seal or cover and refrigerate for 1 hour. Drain and discard marinade. Thread meat on metal or soaked wooden skewers. Grill, uncovered, over medium-hot heat for 6-8 minutes or until juices run clear, turning often. **Yield:** 4 servings.

Nutritional Analysis: One serving (prepared without salt) equals 192 calories, 56 mg sodium, 63 mg cholesterol, 2 gm carbohydrate, 23 gm protein, 9 gm fat. **Diabetic Exchange:** 3-1/2 meat.

Marinated Thanksgiving Turkey

(Pictured below)

Ken Churches, San Andreas, California

My family enjoys this turkey because it cooks up tender, tasty and golden-brown. The marinade flavors the meat very well. I like grilling it since it adds that tempting barbecued flavor.

1-1/2 cups chicken broth
    2 cups water
    1 cup soy sauce
  2/3 cup lemon juice
    2 garlic cloves, minced
1-1/2 teaspoons ground ginger
    1 teaspoon pepper
    1 turkey (12 to 13 pounds)

Combine the first seven ingredients; reserve 1 cup for basting. Pour remaining marinade into a 2-gal. re-

sealable plastic bag. Add the turkey and seal bag; turn to coat. Refrigerate overnight, turning several times.

Drain and discard marinade. Heat grill according to manufacturer's directions for indirect cooking or roast in a conventional oven*. Tuck wings under turkey; place breast side down on grill rack. Cover and grill for 1 hour. Add 10 briquettes to coals; turn the turkey breast side up. Brush with reserved marinade. Cover and cook for 2 hours, adding 10 briquettes to maintain heat and brushing with marinade every 30 minutes until meat thermometer reads 185°. Cover; let stand 20 minutes before carving. **Yield:** 8 servings.

***Conventional Roasting Method:** Place turkey on a rack in a large roaster. Bake, uncovered, at 325° for 4 to 4-1/2 hours or until meat thermometer reads 185°. Baste frequently with reserved marinade. When turkey begins to brown, cover lightly with a tent of aluminum foil.

Campfire Chicken Stew

Florence Kreis, Beach Park, Illinois

My family loves it when I prepare these chicken stew packets on camping trips, but they're equally good on our backyard grill.

> 1 broiler/fryer chicken (3-1/2 to 4 pounds),
>   cut up
> 3 to 4 medium potatoes, peeled and sliced
> 1 cup thinly sliced carrots
> 1 medium green pepper, sliced
> 1 can (10-3/4 ounces) condensed cream of
>   mushroom soup, undiluted
> 1/4 cup water
> 1/2 teaspoon salt
> 1/4 teaspoon pepper

Grill the chicken, uncovered, over medium heat for 3 minutes on each side. Place two pieces of chicken each on four pieces of heavy-duty foil (about 18 in. x 12 in.). Divide the potatoes, carrots and green pepper between the four pieces of foil. Top each with 2 tablespoons soup, 1 tablespoon water, salt and pepper.

Fold the foil around the mixture and seal tightly. Grill, covered, over medium heat for 20 minutes; turn and grill 20-25 minutes longer or until the vegetables are tender and the chicken juices run clear. **Yield:** 4 servings.

Pizza on the Grill

(Pictured above)

Lisa Boettcher, Columbus, Wisconsin

Pizza is such a favorite, I make it once a week. The barbecue flavor mingling with the cheese in this recipe is delicious.

> 1 package (1/4 ounce) active dry yeast
> 1 cup warm water (110° to 115°)
> 2 tablespoons vegetable oil
> 2 teaspoons sugar
> 1 teaspoon baking soda
> 1 teaspoon salt
> 2-3/4 to 3 cups all-purpose flour
>   2 cups cubed cooked chicken
>   1/2 to 3/4 cup barbecue sauce
>   1/2 cup julienned green pepper
>   2 cups (8 ounces) shredded Monterey Jack
>   cheese

In a mixing bowl, dissolve yeast in water. Add the oil, sugar, baking soda, salt and 2 cups flour. Stir in enough remaining flour to form a soft dough. Turn onto a floured surface; knead until smooth and elastic, about 6-8 minutes. Cover and let rest for 10 minutes.

On a floured surface, roll dough into a 13-in. circle. Transfer to a greased 12-in. pizza pan. Build up edges slightly. Grill, covered, over medium heat for 5 minutes. Remove from grill. Combine chicken and barbecue sauce; spread over the crust. Sprinkle with green pepper and cheese. Grill, covered, 5-10 minutes longer or until crust is golden and cheese is melted. **Yield:** 4 servings.

Spicy Grilled Chicken

(Pictured below)

Edith Maki, Hancock, Michigan

Very near the top of the list of foods I prepare for company is this chicken. It is a family favorite, too—any leftovers are great in a salad or sandwich.

- 3/4 cup finely chopped onion
- 1/2 cup grapefruit juice
- 2 tablespoons olive *or* vegetable oil
- 2 tablespoons soy sauce
- 1 tablespoon honey
- 1 garlic clove, minced
- 1-1/2 teaspoons salt
- 1-1/2 teaspoons rubbed sage
- 1-1/2 teaspoons dried thyme
- 1 teaspoon ground allspice
- 1 teaspoon garlic powder
- 1/2 teaspoon ground cinnamon
- 1/2 teaspoon ground nutmeg
- 1/4 teaspoon cayenne pepper
- 1/4 teaspoon pepper
- 6 boneless skinless chicken breast halves (1-1/2 pounds)

In a large resealable plastic bag or shallow glass container, combine the first 15 ingredients; mix well. Re-

serve 1/3 cup for basting and refrigerate. Add chicken to remaining marinade and turn to coat. Seal bag or cover container; refrigerate overnight.

Drain and discard marinade. Grill chicken, uncovered, over medium heat for 3 minutes on each side. Baste with reserved marinade. Continue grilling for 6-8 minutes or until juices run clear, basting and turning several times. **Yield:** 6 servings.

Grilled Chicken Cordon Bleu

(Pictured above)

Shawna McCutcheon, Homer City, Pennsylvania

These special chicken bundles are absolutely delicious. You can assemble them up to 8 hours in advance and keep them in the fridge. Then just place them on the grill shortly before dinner.

6 boneless skinless chicken breast halves
  (1-1/2 pounds)
6 slices Swiss cheese
6 thin slices deli ham
3 tablespoons olive *or* vegetable oil
3/4 cup seasoned bread crumbs

Flatten the chicken to 1/4-in. thickness. Place a slice of cheese and ham on each to within 1/4 in. of edges. Fold in half; secure with thin metal skewers or toothpicks. Brush with oil and roll in bread crumbs. Grill, covered, over medium-hot heat for 15-18 minutes or until juices run clear. **Yield:** 6 servings.

Curry Grilled Chicken

(Pictured below)

Nancy Ode, Sherman, South Dakota

Chicken marinated in this mixture comes out tender and tangy. Its mild curry flavor is equally good on pork, but I marinate it for an hour longer for the best results.

1/2 cup sugar
1/2 cup vinegar
1/3 cup ketchup
  1 tablespoon Worcestershire sauce
1/2 teaspoon ground mustard
1/2 teaspoon paprika

1/2 teaspoon curry powder
1/2 teaspoon garlic salt
1/2 teaspoon salt
1/8 teaspoon pepper
  4 boneless skinless chicken breast halves
    (1-1/4 pounds)

In a blender, combine the first 10 ingredients; cover and process until blended. Pour into a large resealable plastic bag or shallow glass container; add the chicken. Seal or cover and refrigerate for 1-2 hours. Drain and discard marinade. Grill the chicken, covered, over medium heat for 6 minutes on each side or until juices run clear. **Yield:** 4 servings.

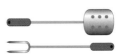

Moist Lemon Chicken

Nancy Schickling, Bedford, Virginia

I originally developed this marinade for seafood, but it's wonderful with chicken, too. It adds mild lemon zing and keeps the meat moist and tender.

 Uses less fat, sugar or salt. Includes Nutritional Analysis and Diabetic Exchanges.

3/4 cup water
1/4 cup lemon juice
  2 tablespoons dried minced onion
  1 tablespoon dried parsley flakes
  1 tablespoon Worcestershire sauce
  2 garlic cloves, minced
  1 teaspoon dill seed
1/2 teaspoon salt, optional
1/2 teaspoon curry powder
1/2 teaspoon pepper
  1 broiler/fryer chicken (3 to 3-1/2 pounds),
    cut up

In a large resealable plastic bag or shallow glass dish, combine the first 10 ingredients. Add chicken and turn to coat. Cover and refrigerate for 4-6 hours. Drain, discarding marinade. Grill chicken, covered, over indirect low heat for 50-60 minutes or until juices run clear, turning several times. **Yield:** 4 servings.

Nutritional Analysis: One serving (prepared with reduced-sodium Worcestershire sauce and without salt) equals 219 calories, 132 mg sodium, 96 mg cholesterol, 3 gm carbohydrate, 36 gm protein, 6 gm fat. **Diabetic Exchange:** 4 lean meat.

bag and turn to coat. Place the peppers, zucchini, pineapple and oranges in another resealable bag; add remaining marinade. Seal bag and turn to coat. Refrigerate chicken and vegetables for 8 hours or overnight, turning occasionally.

Drain chicken, discarding marinade. Drain vegetables and fruits, reserving marinade for basting. Grill the chicken, vegetables and fruits, uncovered, over medium heat for 3 minutes on each side. Baste with reserved marinade. Continue turning and basting 6-8 minutes longer or until chicken juices run clear, vegetables are tender and fruits are golden brown. **Yield:** 6 servings.

Nutritional Analysis: One serving (1 chicken breast with 3/4 cup vegetable mixture) equals 320 calories, 5 g fat (1 g saturated fat), 73 mg cholesterol, 71 mg sodium, 40 g carbohydrate, 4 g fiber, 29 g protein. **Diabetic Exchanges:** 3-1/2 very lean meat, 2 vegetable, 2 fruit, 1/2 fat.

Orange Chicken and Veggies

(Pictured above)

Violet Klause, Onoway, Alberta

A mild maple marinade seasons the chicken, vegetables and fruit in this summery supper.

 Uses less fat, sugar or salt. Includes Nutritional Analysis and Diabetic Exchanges.

- 1 can (6 ounces) frozen orange juice concentrate, thawed
- 3/4 cup maple syrup
- 4 teaspoons canola oil
- 3/4 teaspoon curry powder
- 1/4 teaspoon cayenne pepper
- 6 boneless skinless chicken breast halves (1-1/2 pounds)
- 2 medium sweet red peppers, halved and seeded
- 1 medium green pepper, halved and seeded
- 3 medium zucchini, halved lengthwise
- 1 fresh pineapple, peeled and cut into 1/2-inch slices
- 2 unpeeled medium oranges, cut into 1/2-inch slices

In a bowl, combine the orange juice concentrate, syrup, oil, curry and cayenne. Place chicken in a large resealable plastic bag; add half of the marinade. Seal

Peanut Butter Chicken Skewers

(Pictured below)

Jeanne Bennett, North Richland Hills, Texas

Most people associate peanut butter with snacks or desserts. This fantastic dish proves it also makes a mouth-watering sauce for chicken.

Pineapple Chicken Salad

(Pictured at left)

Stephanie Moon, Green Bay, Wisconsin

Although I love to cook, I appreciate recipes that have me out of the kitchen so I can spend time with my family. We love this main-dish salad. While the chicken's grilling, I prepare the dressing and vegetables.

      4 boneless skinless chicken breast halves
          (1-1/4 pounds)
  1/4 teaspoon lemon-pepper seasoning
      1 can (8 ounces) unsweetened sliced
          pineapple
      3 tablespoons vegetable oil
      2 tablespoons soy sauce
      1 tablespoon vinegar
      1 tablespoon honey
  1/4 teaspoon ground ginger
      8 cups assorted vegetables (lettuce, red
          onion, carrots, sweet red pepper and
          broccoli)
Salted peanuts, optional

Sprinkle chicken with lemon-pepper. Grill over medium-hot heat for 15-18 minutes or until juices run clear, turning once. Set aside and keep warm.

Drain pineapple, reserving 2 tablespoons juice (discard remaining juice or save for another use); set pineapple aside. In a jar with a tight-fitting lid, combine oil, soy sauce, vinegar, honey, ginger and reserved pineapple juice; shake well. Brush some of the dressing over pineapple; grill for 2 minutes.

Cut chicken into strips. Arrange vegetables on serving plates; top with pineapple and chicken. Sprinkle with peanuts if desired. Serve with remaining dressing. **Yield:** 4 servings.

  1/2 cup creamy peanut butter
  1/2 cup water
  1/4 cup soy sauce
      4 garlic cloves, minced
      3 tablespoons lemon juice
      2 tablespoons brown sugar
  3/4 teaspoon ground ginger
  1/2 teaspoon crushed red pepper flakes
      4 boneless skinless chicken breast halves
          (1-1/4 pounds)
      2 cups shredded red cabbage
Sliced green onion tops

In a saucepan, combine the first eight ingredients; cook and stir over medium-high heat for 5 minutes or until smooth.

Reserve half of the sauce. Slice chicken lengthwise into 1-in. strips; thread onto metal or soaked wooden skewers.

Grill, uncovered, over medium-hot heat for 2 minutes; turn and brush with peanut butter sauce. Continue turning and basting for 4-6 minutes or until juices run clear.

Place cabbage on a serving plate; top with chicken. Sprinkle with onion tops. Serve with reserved sauce. **Yield:** 4 servings.

Preventing Flareups

FORESTALL FLAREUPS in one of several ways.

Before beginning to grill, trim excess fat from meats or use lean ground meats, or place a drip pan immediately beneath meats, stacking coals on either side.

If you don't have a drip pan, make one out of foil. Tear off a piece of heavy-duty foil that's twice the length of your grill, then fold it in half crosswise. Bend all the edges up 1-1/2 inches. Fold the corners to the inside to reinforce them.

Green Chili Chicken Sandwiches

(Pictured below)

Paula Morigeau, Hot Springs, Montana

I enjoyed a sandwich similar to this in a restaurant and decided to try making it at home. The spicy chicken is a quick-and-easy alternative to hamburgers when entertaining outdoors.

- 4 boneless skinless chicken breast halves (1-1/4 pounds)
- 2/3 cup soy sauce
- 1/4 cup cider vinegar
- 2 tablespoons sugar
- 2 teaspoons vegetable oil
- 1 can (4 ounces) whole green chilies, drained and sliced lengthwise
- 4 slices Pepper Jack *or* Monterey Jack cheese
- 4 kaiser *or* sandwich rolls, split

Pound chicken to flatten; place in a large resealable plastic bag. In a bowl, combine the soy sauce, vinegar, sugar and oil; mix well. Set aside 1/4 cup for basting. Pour the remaining marinade over chicken; seal bag and turn to coat. Refrigerate for 30 minutes.

Drain and discard marinade. Grill chicken, uncovered, over medium heat for 3 minutes. Turn and

baste with reserved marinade; grill 3 minutes longer or until juices run clear. Top each with a green chili and cheese slice; cover and grill for 2 minutes or until cheese is melted. Serve on rolls. **Yield:** 4 servings.

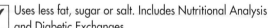

Cool Cucumber Chicken

(Pictured above)

Andria Barosi-Stampone, Randolph, New Jersey

My husband really likes chicken, so when I need a delicious dish for a picnic or barbecue, this is what I make.

 Uses less fat, sugar or salt. Includes Nutritional Analysis and Diabetic Exchanges.

- 4 boneless skinless chicken breast halves (1-1/4 pounds)
- 2 tablespoons olive *or* vegetable oil
- 1 medium cucumber, seeded and chopped
- 1/2 cup plain reduced-fat yogurt
- 2 tablespoons reduced-fat mayonnaise
- 1 tablespoon minced fresh dill
- 1/8 teaspoon pepper

Brush both sides of chicken with oil. Grill over medium heat, turning occasionally, for 10-14 minutes or until juices run clear. Meanwhile, combine remaining ingredients in a small bowl. Spoon over warm chicken; serve immediately. Or, to serve cold, spoon sauce over chicken and refrigerate several hours or overnight. **Yield:** 4 servings.

Nutritional Analysis: One serving equals 256 calories, 134 mg sodium, 75 mg cholesterol, 7 gm carbohydrate, 29 gm protein, 12 gm fat. **Diabetic Exchanges:** 4 very lean meat, 1-1/2 fat, 1 vegetable.

Maple-Glazed Chicken Wings

(Pictured below)

Janice Henck, Clarkston, Georgia

Some wonderful maple syrup I brought back from my last trip to Vermont inspired this recipe. These wings have been a hit with family and friends.

    2 to 3 pounds whole chicken wings
    1 cup maple syrup
    2/3 cup chili sauce
    1/2 cup finely chopped onion
    2 tablespoons Dijon mustard
    2 teaspoons Worcestershire sauce
    1/4 to 1/2 teaspoon crushed red pepper flakes

Cut chicken wings into three sections; discard wing tip section. In a large resealable plastic bag or shallow glass container, combine remaining ingredients. Re-

serve 1 cup for basting and refrigerate. Add chicken to remaining marinade and turn to coat. Seal bag or cover container; refrigerate for 4 hours, turning occasionally. Drain and discard marinade.

Grill chicken, covered, over medium heat for 12-16 minutes, turning occasionally. Brush with reserved marinade. Grill, uncovered, for 8-10 minutes or until juices run clear, basting and turning several times. **Yield:** 6-8 servings.

Apricot-Stuffed Turkey Breast

Bonnie De Meyer, New Carlisle, Indiana

For a new take on turkey, give this recipe a try. It cooks on the grill, and it's stuffed with a sensational apricot mixture.

 Uses less fat, sugar or salt. Includes Nutritional Analysis and Diabetic Exchanges.

    1 bone-in turkey breast half (2-1/2 pounds), skin removed
1-1/2 cups soft bread crumbs
    1/2 cup diced dried apricots
    1/4 cup chopped pecans, toasted
    3 tablespoons water *or* unsweetened apple juice, *divided*
    1 tablespoon vegetable oil
    1/4 teaspoon dried rosemary, crushed
    1/4 teaspoon garlic salt
    1 tablespoon Dijon mustard

Remove bone from turkey. Cut a horizontal slit into thickest part of turkey to form a 5-in. x 4-in. pocket. In a bowl, combine the bread crumbs, apricots, pecans, 2 tablespoons water or juice, oil, rosemary and garlic salt; toss gently. Stuff into pocket of turkey. Secure opening with metal or soaked wooden skewers.

Grill, covered, over indirect heat for 30 minutes. Combine the mustard and remaining water; brush over the turkey. Grill 10 minutes longer or until golden brown and a meat thermometer inserted into the stuffing reads 165°. Let stand 10 minutes before slicing. **Yield:** 8 servings.

Nutritional Analysis: One serving (calculated with water instead of apple juice) equals 268 calories, 313 mg sodium, 81 mg cholesterol, 20 gm carbohydrate, 33 gm protein, 6 gm fat, 2 gm fiber. **Diabetic Exchanges:** 4 very lean meat, 1 starch, 1/2 fruit, 1/2 fat.

Grilled Chicken Dinner

Floyd Hulet, Apache Junction, Arizona

This complete meal grilled in a foil packet is a palate-pleasing and mess-free dinner for one.

> 1 bone-in chicken breast half
> 1 medium potato, peeled and quartered
> 1 large carrot, cut into 2-inch pieces
> 1/2 cup fresh vegetables (broccoli florets, peas *and/or* green beans)
> 1 tablespoon onion soup mix
> 2/3 cup condensed cream of chicken soup, undiluted

Place chicken in the center of a piece of double-layered heavy-duty foil (about 18 in. square). Place vegetables around chicken. Sprinkle with soup mix. Top with soup. Fold foil around vegetables and chicken and seal tightly.

Grill, uncovered, over medium-low heat for 50-60 minutes or until chicken juices run clear and potato is tender. Open foil carefully to allow steam to escape. **Yield:** 1 serving.

Jalapeno Grilled Chicken

(Pictured at right)

Cheryl Kvintus, Altus, Oklahoma

I've had this recipe for years, so it's long been a family favorite. The jalapeno stuffing adds some spice to ordinary grilled chicken.

> 4 to 8 jalapeno peppers, seeded and chopped* *or* 1 can (4 ounces) chopped green chilies
> 2/3 cup lemon juice, *divided*
> 1/4 cup minced fresh parsley *or* 1 tablespoon dried parsley flakes
> 6 to 10 garlic cloves, minced
> 2 teaspoons dried rosemary, crushed
> 2 teaspoons dried thyme
> 8 bone-in chicken breast halves
> 2/3 cup chicken broth
> 2 teaspoons pepper
> 1/2 teaspoon grated lemon peel

In a bowl, combine the peppers, 1/3 cup lemon juice, parsley, garlic, rosemary and thyme. Gently stuff pepper mixture under the skin of each chicken breast.

Barbecued Turkey Slices

(Pictured above)

Jerry Olson, Ephraim, Utah

At banquets, church dinners and even wedding buffets, this tantalizing turkey is a "must" for the table. It was a hit with the 100-plus guests at our family reunion. I've served it with cheesy potatoes and assorted summer salads. It's a snap to fix ahead of time and keeps well in the freezer.

> 1/2 cup grapefruit *or* citrus soda
> 1/2 cup soy sauce
> 1/4 cup vegetable oil
> 2-1/2 teaspoons garlic powder
> 1 teaspoon prepared horseradish
> 2-1/2 pounds boneless skinless turkey breast, cut into 3/4-inch slices

In a large resealable plastic bag, combine the soda, soy sauce, oil, garlic powder and horseradish. Add turkey slices. Seal bag and turn to coat; refrigerate for 6-8 hours or overnight.

Drain and discard the marinade. Grill the turkey, uncovered, over medium heat for 4-5 minutes on each side or until the turkey juices run clear. **Yield:** 8-10 servings.

Place in a greased 13-in. x 9-in. x 2-in. baking dish. Combine the broth, pepper, lemon peel and remaining lemon juice; pour over chicken. Cover and refrigerate for at least 6 hours.

Drain and discard marinade. Place chicken skin side up on grill. Grill, covered, over medium heat for 45 minutes or until juices run clear, turning once. **Yield:** 8 servings.

Editor's Note: When cutting or seeding hot peppers, use rubber or plastic gloves to protect your hands. Avoid touching your face.

Sesame Ginger Chicken

(Pictured at right)

Nancy Johnson, Connersville, Indiana

Why grill plain chicken breasts when a simple ginger-honey basting sauce can make them extra special? This tempting chicken is a wonderful summer main dish since it's quick and light. We love it.

2 tablespoons soy sauce
2 tablespoons honey
1 tablespoon sesame seeds, toasted
1/2 teaspoon ground ginger
4 boneless skinless chicken breast halves
(1-1/4 pounds)
2 green onions with tops, cut into thin strips

In a small bowl, combine the first four ingredients; set aside. Pound the chicken breasts to 1/4-in. thickness. Grill over medium-hot heat, turning and basting frequently with soy sauce mixture, for 8 minutes or until juices run clear. Garnish with onions. **Yield:** 4 servings.

Cooking Chicken

BOTH under- and overcooking result in a tough chicken. For the most tender results, cook boneless skinless chicken breast halves to an internal temperature of 170°.

Bone-in chicken parts should read 170° for white meat and 180° for dark meat.

Grilled Chicken Over Spinach

(Pictured below)

Michelle Krzmarzick, Redondo Beach, California

With two young children to keep me busy, it's essential to have a few speedy dishes for days when I'm short on time. This recipe is one I've pieced together and added my own touches to.

 Uses less fat, sugar or salt. Includes Nutritional Analysis and Diabetic Exchanges.

- 1 to 2 tablespoons olive *or* canola oil
- 1 tablespoon cider vinegar
- 1 garlic clove, minced
- 1 teaspoon dried thyme
- 1/2 teaspoon dried oregano
- 1/2 teaspoon cayenne pepper
- 1/4 teaspoon salt
- Dash pepper
- 4 boneless skinless chicken breast halves (1-1/4 pounds)

SAUTEED SPINACH:
- 1 green onion, finely chopped
- 1 to 2 garlic cloves, minced
- 1 to 2 tablespoons olive *or* canola oil
- 1/2 pound fresh mushrooms, sliced
- 1 package (10 ounces) fresh spinach, torn

In a bowl, combine the first eight ingredients; mix well. Spoon over chicken. Grill, uncovered, over medium heat for 7 minutes on each side or until juices run clear.

In a large skillet, saute onion and garlic in oil for 1 minute. Stir in mushrooms; saute for 3-4 minutes or until tender. Add spinach; saute for 2 minutes or until wilted. Transfer to a serving platter; top with chicken. **Yield:** 4 servings.

Nutritional Analysis: One serving (prepared with a total of 2 tablespoons oil) equals 237 calories, 10 g fat (2 g saturated fat), 73 mg cholesterol, 268 mg sodium, 6 g carbohydrate, 3 g fiber, 31 g protein. **Diabetic Exchanges:** 3-1/2 lean meat, 1 vegetable.

Barbecued Hot Wings

(Pictured above)

Anita Carr, Cadiz, Ohio

My husband can't get enough of these spicy chicken wings. They're excellent appetizers at cookouts. We serve them with blue cheese dressing and celery sticks.

- 12 whole chicken wings (about 2-1/2 pounds)*
- 1 bottle (8 ounces) Italian salad dressing
- 1/2 to 3/4 cup hot pepper sauce
- 1/8 to 1/2 teaspoon cayenne pepper
- 2 tablespoons butter *or* margarine, melted

Cut chicken wings into three sections; discard wing tips. In a bowl, combine salad dressing, hot pepper sauce and cayenne. Remove 1/2 cup for basting; cover and refrigerate. Place remaining sauce in a large resealable plastic bag or shallow glass dish; add chicken and turn to coat. Seal or cover and refrigerate overnight. Drain and discard the marinade.

Grill wings, covered, over medium heat for 12-16 minutes, turning occasionally. Add butter to the reserved sauce; brush over wings. Grill, uncovered, 8-10 minutes longer or until juices run clear, basting and turning several times. **Yield:** 6-8 servings.

*Editor's Note: 2-1/2 pounds of uncooked chicken wing sections may be substituted for the whole chicken wings. Omit the first step of the recipe.

Herbed Chicken Quarters

(Pictured below)

Erika Aylward, Clinton, Michigan

I often grill chicken in the summer, and this herbed version is a big hit with our three daughters. Garlic, basil, thyme, salt and cayenne pepper perfectly season the chicken pieces. A salad and seasoned potatoes make scrumptious complements to the plump, juicy chicken.

>   4 medium lemons, cut into wedges
> 1/2 cup vegetable oil
>   8 garlic cloves, minced
>   4 teaspoons minced fresh basil
>   2 teaspoons minced fresh thyme
>   2 teaspoons salt
> 1/2 teaspoon cayenne pepper
>   1 broiler/fryer chicken (about 3 pounds), quartered

Gently squeeze the juice from the lemons into a large resealable plastic bag; leave the lemon wedges in the bag. Add the oil, garlic, basil, thyme, salt and cayenne. Add the chicken and turn to coat. Seal bag and refrigerate for 24 hours, turning frequently.

Drain and discard the marinade. Grill chicken, covered, over medium heat, turning every 15 minutes, for 1 hour or until a meat thermometer reads 170° for breast meat quarters and 180° for leg quarters. **Yield:** 4 servings.

Chicken Broccoli Packets

Lynda Simmons, Fayetteville, North Carolina

I like this recipe because it's simple to prepare and cleanup is a snap! I just put some chicken and veggies in a foil packet, then pop them on the grill. The packets can serve as serving plates.

>   4 boneless skinless chicken breast halves (1-1/4 pounds)
> Seasoned salt
>   1 package (10 ounces) frozen broccoli spears
>   1 medium onion, sliced into rings
>   4 teaspoons lemon juice
>   4 tablespoons butter *or* margarine

Place each chicken breast in the center of a piece of heavy-duty foil (about 12 in. x 12 in.). Sprinkle with seasoned salt. Top each with 2 broccoli spears, 3-4 onion rings, 1 teaspoon lemon juice and 1 tablespoon butter. Fold foil around chicken; seal tightly.

Grill, covered, over medium-hot heat for 20 minutes or until meat juices run clear. Serve in foil packets if desired. **Yield:** 4 servings.

Tropical Island Chicken

(Pictured above)

Sharon Hanson, Franklin, Tennessee

The marinade makes a savory statement in this all-time-favorite chicken recipe that I served at our son's pirate-theme birthday party. The aroma was so good on the grill that guests could hardly wait to try a piece!

     1/2 cup soy sauce
     1/3 cup vegetable oil
     1/4 cup water
       2 tablespoons dried minced onion
       2 tablespoons sesame seeds
       1 tablespoon sugar
       4 garlic cloves, minced
       1 teaspoon ground ginger
     3/4 teaspoon salt
     1/8 teaspoon cayenne pepper
       2 broiler/fryer chickens (3 to 4 pounds *each*), quartered

In a large resealable plastic bag, combine the first 10 ingredients. Remove 1/3 cup for basting; cover and refrigerate. Add chicken to bag; seal and turn to coat. Refrigerate for 8 hours or overnight.

Drain and discard marinade. Grill chicken, covered, over medium-hot heat for 45-60 minutes or until a meat thermometer reads 170° for breast meat quarters and 180° for leg quarters, turning and basting often with reserved marinade. **Yield:** 8 servings.

Grilled Turkey Breast

(Pictured below)

Ravonda Mormann, Raleigh, North Carolina

I combined several recipes to come up with this entree that our family loves any time of year. After marinating overnight, the turkey is grilled, then dressed up with a fast fruity sauce.

 Uses less fat, sugar or salt. Includes Nutritional Analysis and Diabetic Exchanges.

       2 boneless skinless turkey breast halves
         (about 2-1/2 pounds *each*)
       1 cup cranberry juice
     1/4 cup orange juice
     1/4 cup olive *or* vegetable oil
       1 teaspoon salt, optional
       1 teaspoon pepper
SAUCE:
       1 can (16 ounces) jellied cranberry sauce
     1/4 cup lemon juice
       3 tablespoons brown sugar
       1 teaspoon cornstarch

Place turkey in a large resealable plastic bag. Combine the next five ingredients; pour over turkey. Seal and refrigerate for 8 hours or overnight, turning occasionally.

Drain and discard marinade. Grill turkey, covered, over indirect heat for 1-1/4 to 1-1/2 hours or until

1/2 teaspoon salt
2 dashes hot pepper sauce
2 broiler/fryer chickens (3-1/2 to 4 pounds *each*), quartered

In a saucepan, saute the garlic in butter until tender. Add the next eight ingredients. Bring to a boil, stirring constantly. Remove from the heat and set aside.

Grill the chicken, covered, over medium heat for 30 minutes, turning occasionally. Baste with sauce. Grill 15 minutes longer or until a meat thermometer reads 170° for breast meat quarters or 180° for leg quarters, basting and turning several times. **Yield:** 8 servings.

Grilled Turkey Tenderloin

(Pictured on page 28)

Denise Nebel, Wayland, Iowa

When they taste my grilled specialty, guests say, "This turkey melts in your mouth—and the flavor is fantastic!" The recipe includes a tangy marinade that was developed for our turkey producers' booth at the state fair one summer.

✓ Uses less fat, sugar or salt. Includes Nutritional Analysis and Diabetic Exchanges.

1/4 cup soy sauce
1/4 cup vegetable oil
1/4 cup apple juice
2 tablespoons lemon juice
2 tablespoons dried minced onion
1 teaspoon vanilla extract
1/4 teaspoon ground ginger
Dash *each* garlic powder and pepper
2 turkey breast tenderloins (1/2 pound *each*)

In a large resealable plastic bag or shallow glass dish, combine the soy sauce, oil, apple juice, lemon juice, onion, vanilla, ginger, garlic powder and pepper. Add turkey; seal or cover and refrigerate for at least 2 hours. Drain and discard marinade. Grill turkey, covered, over medium heat for 8-10 minutes per side or until juices run clear. **Yield:** 4 servings.

Nutritional Analysis: One serving (prepared with reduced-sodium soy sauce) equals 284 calories, 558 mg sodium, 82 mg cholesterol, 6 gm carbohydrate, 31 gm protein, 14 gm fat. **Diabetic Exchanges:** 4 lean meat, 1 vegetable, 1/2 fat.

juices run clear and a meat thermometer reads 170°. Meanwhile, combine sauce ingredients in a saucepan; cook and stir over medium heat until thickened, about 5 minutes. Serve with the turkey. **Yield:** 10 servings.

Nutritional Analysis: One serving (prepared with unsweetened cranberry and orange juices; calculated without the sauce) equals 110 calories, 149 mg sodium, 51 mg cholesterol, 1 gm carbohydrate, 18 gm protein, 3 gm fat. **Diabetic Exchange:** 2 very lean meat.

Barbecued Picnic Chicken

(Pictured above)

Priscilla Weaver, Hagerstown, Maryland

When we entertain friends at our cabin, I like to serve this savory chicken. Cooked on a covered grill, the poultry stays so tender and juicy. Everyone loves the zesty, slightly sweet homemade barbecue sauce.

2 garlic cloves, minced
2 teaspoons butter *or* margarine
1 cup ketchup
1/4 cup packed brown sugar
1/4 cup chili sauce
2 tablespoons Worcestershire sauce
1 tablespoon celery seed
1 tablespoon prepared mustard

Herb Fryer Chicken

(Pictured below)

Charlene Sylvia, Sandy, Utah

We use our grill all year long. Our boys love this chicken, and it's a hit with company, too. To really bring out the lemon flavor, pierce the chicken skin before marinating the meat overnight.

      1/3 cup lemon juice
      1/4 cup olive *or* vegetable oil
      1/4 cup minced fresh parsley
         2 tablespoons finely chopped onion
         3 garlic cloves, minced
         1 tablespoon grated lemon peel
         1 teaspoon minced fresh thyme
      1/2 teaspoon salt
      1/4 teaspoon pepper
         1 broiler/fryer chicken (3 pounds), cut up

In a large resealable plastic bag, combine the lemon juice, oil, parsley, onion, garlic, lemon peel, thyme, salt and pepper; add chicken. Seal bag and turn to coat; refrigerate overnight, turning occasionally. Drain and discard marinade.

Grill chicken, covered, over medium heat for 35-40 minutes or until juices run clear, turning every 15 minutes. **Yield:** 6 servings.

Jalapeno Chicken Wraps

(Pictured above)

Leslie Buenz, Tinley Park, Illinois

These easy appetizers are always a hit at parties! Zesty strips of chicken and bits of onion sit in jalapeno halves that are wrapped in bacon and grilled. Serve them with blue cheese or ranch salad dressing for dipping.

         1 pound boneless skinless chicken breasts
         1 tablespoon garlic powder
         1 tablespoon onion powder
         1 tablespoon pepper
         2 teaspoons seasoned salt
         1 teaspoon paprika
         1 small onion, cut into strips
       15 jalapeno peppers, halved and seeded*
         1 pound sliced bacon, halved widthwise
Blue cheese salad dressing

Cut chicken into 2-in. x 1-1/2-in. strips. In a large resealable plastic bag, combine the garlic powder, onion powder, pepper, seasoned salt and paprika; add chicken and shake to coat. Place a chicken and onion strip in each jalapeno half. Wrap each with a piece of bacon and secure with toothpicks.

Grill, uncovered, over indirect medium heat for 18-20 minutes or until chicken juices run clear and bacon is crisp, turning once. Serve with blue cheese dressing. **Yield:** 2-1/2 dozen.

*Editor's Note: When cutting or seeding hot peppers, use rubber or plastic gloves to protect your hands. Avoid touching your face.

Chicken Pizza Packets

(Pictured below)

Amber Zurbrugg, Alliance, Ohio

Basil, garlic, pepperoni and mozzarella give plenty of pizza flavor to chicken, green pepper, zucchini and cherry tomatoes in these individual foil dinners. This speedy grilled supper is a tasty way to get little ones to eat their veggies.

    1 pound boneless skinless chicken breasts, cut
      into 1-inch pieces
    2 tablespoons olive *or* vegetable oil
    1 small zucchini, thinly sliced
   16 pepperoni slices
    1 small green pepper, julienned
    1 small onion, sliced
  1/2 teaspoon dried oregano
  1/2 teaspoon dried basil
  1/4 teaspoon salt
  1/4 teaspoon garlic powder
  1/4 teaspoon pepper
    1 cup halved cherry tomatoes
  1/2 cup shredded mozzarella cheese
  1/2 cup shredded Parmesan cheese

In a large bowl, combine the first 11 ingredients. Coat four pieces of heavy-duty foil (about 12 in. square)

with nonstick cooking spray. Place a quarter of the chicken mixture in the center of each piece. Fold foil around mixture and seal tightly. Grill, covered, over medium-hot heat for 15-18 minutes or until chicken juices run clear.

Carefully open each packet. Sprinkle with tomatoes and mozzarella and Parmesan cheeses. Seal packet loosely; grill 2 minutes longer or until cheese is melted. **Yield:** 4 servings.

Cranberry Turkey Cutlets

Marguerite Shaeffer, Sewell, New Jersey

When our son-in-law brought home some wild turkey one year, we turned to this recipe. He took care of the grilling while I made the sauce, and we all enjoyed this healthy entree.

 Uses less fat, sugar or salt. Includes Nutritional Analysis and Diabetic Exchanges.

      1 cup thinly sliced onion
      2 teaspoons vegetable *or* canola oil
      2 cups dried cranberries
      2 cups orange juice
  1-1/2 teaspoons balsamic vinegar *or* cider
        vinegar
      6 turkey cutlets (4 ounces *each* and
        1/2 inch thick)
    1/2 teaspoon salt
    1/2 teaspoon pepper

In a large skillet, saute onion in oil until lightly browned, about 6 minutes. Stir in the cranberries, orange juice and vinegar. Bring to a boil over medium heat; cook and stir until sauce begins to thicken. Set aside.

Coat grill rack with nonstick cooking spray before starting the grill. Sprinkle the turkey cutlets with salt and pepper. Grill, covered, over indirect medium heat for 5-6 minutes on each side or until turkey juices run clear.

Top each cutlet with some of the cranberry sauce; grill 1-2 minutes longer. Serve with remaining cranberry sauce. **Yield:** 6 servings.

Nutritional Analysis: One serving (1 cutlet with 1/3 cup cranberry sauce) equals 309 calories, 2 g fat (trace saturated fat), 70 mg cholesterol, 252 mg sodium, 40 g carbohydrate, 4 g fiber, 29 g protein. **Diabetic Exchanges:** 3 very lean meat, 1-1/2 starch, 1 fruit.

Pork, Ham and Sausage

Grilled Rosemary Pork Roast (p. 57)

Chapter 3

20 minutes, turning occasionally, until meat juices run clear. To serve, wrap a slice of bread around about five pork cubes and pull off skewer. **Yield:** 12 servings.

Nutritional Analysis: One serving (not including bread) equals 214 calories, 152 mg sodium, 77 mg cholesterol, 1 gm carbohydrate, 24 gm protein, 12 gm fat. **Diabetic Exchange:** 4 lean meat.

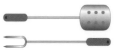

Peanutty Pork Kabobs

(Pictured below)

Ellen Koch, St. Martinville, Louisiana

Cubes of pork tenderloin and green pepper chunks get a spicy treatment from a combination of peanut butter, brown sugar, ginger and red pepper flakes. Reserving half of this mixture to use as a basting sauce adds an extra boost of flavor.

      1/2 cup soy sauce
      1/4 cup lime *or* lemon juice
      1/4 cup peanut butter
      2 tablespoons brown sugar
      2 garlic cloves, minced

Pork Spiedis

(Pictured above)

Beatrice Riddell, Chenango Bridge, New York

Spiedis (pronounced "speed-eez") are a type of grilled meat sandwich considered a local specialty. This recipe is my own, but there are many variations in our area. In nearby Binghamton, Spiedi-Fest is held in August, featuring this delicious dish made of all different kinds of meat. Thousands of people attend. I hope you enjoy my pork version.

 Uses less fat, sugar or salt. Includes Nutritional Analysis and Diabetic Exchanges.

      4 pounds pork tenderloin, cut into 1-inch
         cubes
      2 cups tomato juice
      2 large onions, finely chopped
      4 to 5 garlic cloves, minced
      2 tablespoons Worcestershire sauce
      2 teaspoons chopped fresh basil *or* 1
         teaspoon dried basil
Pepper to taste
      12 slices Italian bread

In a large bowl, combine the first seven ingredients. Cover and refrigerate overnight. Drain, discarding marinade. Thread pork on small skewers; grill for 15-

1 teaspoon crushed red pepper flakes
1/4 teaspoon ground ginger
1 pork tenderloin (about 1 pound), cut into
1-inch cubes
2 medium green peppers, cut into 1-inch
pieces

In a large bowl, combine the first seven ingredients; mix well. Set aside 1/2 cup for basting; cover and refrigerate. Pour remaining marinade into a large resealable plastic bag or shallow glass container; add pork and turn to coat. Seal or cover and refrigerate for 2-3 hours, turning occasionally.

Drain and discard the marinade. On metal or soaked wooden skewers, alternate pork and green peppers. Grill, uncovered, over medium heat for 6 minutes, turning once. Baste with reserved marinade. Grill 8-10 minutes longer or until meat juices run clear, turning and basting frequently. **Yield:** 4 servings.

Marinated Chops 'n' Onion

Connie Brueggeman, Sparta, Wisconsin

The first time I made this spicy dish, my husband commented on how moist the pork was, so I knew it was a keeper. It gets eye-appeal from red onion slices that turn a pretty pink when they're cooked.

 Uses less fat, sugar or salt. Includes Nutritional Analysis and Diabetic Exchanges.

3/4 cup lime juice
1 teaspoon salt, optional
1/4 to 1/2 teaspoon cayenne pepper
4 pork chops (1/2 inch thick)
1 large red onion, sliced

In a large resealable plastic bag or shallow glass container, combine lime juice, salt if desired and cayenne. Add pork chops and onion; turn to coat. Cover and refrigerate for at least 2 hours.

Drain, reserving marinade and onion. Grill chops, covered, over medium-hot heat for 8-10 minutes on each side or until meat juices run clear. Place the marinade and onion in a saucepan; bring to a rolling boil. Serve with the chops. **Yield:** 4 servings.
Nutritional Analysis: One serving (prepared without salt) equals 171 calories, 45 mg sodium, 59 mg cholesterol, 7 gm carbohydrate, 22 gm protein, 6 gm fat.
Diabetic Exchanges: 3 lean meat, 1/2 fruit.

Barbecued Spareribs

(Pictured above and on front cover)

Jane Uphoff, Idalia, Colorado

All of us—my husband, our two sons and I—love to eat barbecued ribs. But the closest rib restaurant to us is in Denver, which is 150 miles away. So I came up with this recipe. It's now our traditional meal on the Fourth of July.

1 tablespoon ground mustard
1 tablespoon chili powder
1/2 teaspoon cayenne pepper
1/4 teaspoon garlic powder
3 pounds pork spareribs
2/3 cup ketchup
1/2 cup water
1/2 cup chopped onion
1/4 cup lemon juice
2 tablespoons vegetable oil
1 teaspoon dried oregano
1 teaspoon liquid smoke, optional
1/2 teaspoon salt
1/4 teaspoon pepper

Combine the first four ingredients; rub over ribs. For sauce, combine the remaining ingredients; mix well and set aside. Grill ribs, covered, over indirect, medium-low heat for 1 hour, turning occasionally. Add 10 briquettes to coals. Grill 30 minutes longer, basting both sides several times with sauce, or until meat is tender. **Yield:** 4 servings.

Campfire Bundles

(Pictured below)

Lauri Krause, Jackson, Nebraska

A family camping trip's where I "invented" this recipe. I'd brought along a hodgepodge of ingredients, so I just threw them all together in a foil packet. Everyone said that the bundles were delicious. Ever since, I've grilled them at home with equally good results.

- 1 large sweet onion, sliced
- 1 *each* large green, sweet red and yellow peppers, sliced
- 4 medium potatoes, sliced 1/2 inch thick
- 6 medium carrots, sliced 1/4 inch thick
- 1 small cabbage, sliced
- 2 medium tomatoes, chopped
- 1 to 1-1/2 pounds fully cooked Polish sausage, cut into 1/2-inch pieces
- 1/2 cup butter *or* margarine
- 1 teaspoon salt
- 1/2 teaspoon pepper

Place vegetables in order listed on three pieces of double-layered heavy-duty foil (about 18 in. x 18 in.). Add sausage; dot with butter. Sprinkle with salt and pepper. Fold foil around the mixture and seal tightly.

Grill, covered, over medium heat for 30 minutes. Turn and grill 30 minutes longer or until vegetables are tender. **Yield:** 6 servings.

Pork with Tangy Mustard Sauce

(Pictured above and on front cover)

Ginger Johnson, Farmington, Illinois

About any side dish would accompany this entree well. In summer, we like to have our homegrown sweet corn and cheesy potatoes hot off the grill, a cold salad and green vegetables alongside it. If you ever have leftovers—it's rare that we do!—the pork would be good in a breakfast casserole or omelet.

- 1 boneless pork loin roast (2-1/2 to 3 pounds)
- 2 teaspoons olive *or* vegetable oil
- 1-1/4 teaspoons ground mustard
- 3/4 teaspoon garlic powder
- 1/4 teaspoon ground ginger
- 1/2 cup horseradish mustard*
- 1/2 cup apricot *or* pineapple preserves

Rub roast with oil. Combine mustard, garlic powder and ginger; rub over roast. Place in a large resealable plastic bag or shallow glass container; seal bag or cover container. Refrigerate overnight.

Grill roast, covered, over indirect medium heat for 60 minutes. Combine the horseradish mustard and preserves. Continue grilling for 15-30 minutes, basting twice with sauce, or until a meat thermometer reads 160°-170°. Let stand for 10 minutes before slicing. Heat remaining sauce to serve with roast. **Yield:** 10-12 servings.

***Editor's Note:** As a substitute for horseradish mustard, combine 1/4 cup spicy brown mustard and 1/4 cup prepared horseradish.

Grilled Ham Slices

Rita Deere, Evansville, Indiana

A simply spiced marinade gives mild sweet flavor to these tender grilled ham slices. It's very good served with scrambled eggs for brunch. We round out the meal with melon balls and buttered toast.

  2 fully cooked ham slices (about 1 pound each)
  1 cup pineapple juice
  1 cup sherry or apple juice
  1/4 cup butter or margarine, melted
  1 tablespoon ground mustard
  1/4 teaspoon ground cloves

Place ham in a large resealable plastic bag. In a bowl, combine the remaining ingredients; mix well. Remove 1/2 cup for basting; cover and refrigerate. Pour remaining marinade over ham; seal bag and turn to coat. Refrigerate for 8 hours or overnight.

Drain and discard marinade. Grill ham, uncovered, over medium-hot heat for 3-4 minutes on each side until heated through, basting frequently with the reserved marinade. **Yield:** 6 servings.

Grilled Pork with Pear Salsa

(Pictured at right)

Suzan Ward, Coeur d'Alene, Idaho

My husband, Dave, and I have been in a dinner group with three other couples for a few years now. We often share our recipes. The pork was served by one of the couples, and I decided to "pear" it with this fabulous salsa. It's a winning combination.

  1/4 cup lime juice
  2 tablespoons olive or vegetable oil
  2 garlic cloves, minced
1-1/2 teaspoons ground cumin
1-1/2 teaspoons dried oregano
  1/2 teaspoon pepper
  2 pork tenderloins (about 1 pound each), cut into 3/4-inch slices
PEAR SALSA:
  4 cups chopped peeled pears (about 4 medium)
  1/3 cup chopped red onion
  2 tablespoons chopped fresh mint or 2 teaspoons dried mint
  2 tablespoons lime juice
  1 tablespoon grated lime peel
  1 jalapeno pepper, seeded and chopped*
  1 teaspoon sugar
  1/2 teaspoon pepper

In a large resealable plastic bag, combine the lime juice, oil, garlic, cumin, oregano and pepper; add pork. Seal bag and turn to coat; refrigerate overnight.

Drain and discard marinade. Grill pork, uncovered, over indirect medium heat for 6-7 minutes on each side or until meat juices run clear. In a bowl, combine salsa ingredients. Serve with the pork. **Yield:** 6-8 servings.

***Editor's Note:** When cutting or seeding hot peppers, use rubber or plastic gloves to protect your hands. Avoid touching your face.

Marinated Pork Strips

(Pictured above)

Karen Peterson, Hainesville, Illinois

This is a good recipe for grilling, especially if you're having company. While it looks like you spent time on it, it's actually easy to prepare. The meat marinates overnight so all you have to do is put it on the grill.

    5 tablespoons soy sauce
1/4 cup ketchup
    3 tablespoons vinegar
    3 tablespoons chili sauce
    3 tablespoons sugar
    2 teaspoons salt
1/8 teaspoon pepper
    3 garlic cloves, minced
    2 cans (12 ounces *each*) lemon-lime soda
    2 pounds pork tenderloin, cut lengthwise into
       1/2-inch strips

In a large bowl, combine the first nine ingredients. Place pork in a heavy resealable plastic bag; add the marinade. Seal the bag and turn to coat. Refrigerate overnight.

Drain and discard marinade. Thread pork onto metal or soaked wooden skewers. Grill over hot heat for 12 minutes, turning once, or until meat juices run clear. **Yield:** 6-8 servings.

Kielbasa Apple Kabobs

(Pictured below)

Edna Hoffman, Hebron, Indiana

Sausage makes these colorful kabobs different from most. The meaty chunks are skewered with tart apples and colorful peppers, then basted with a mild sweet glaze.

 Uses less fat, sugar or salt. Includes Nutritional Analysis and Diabetic Exchanges.

1/4 cup sugar
    1 tablespoon cornstarch
3/4 cup cranberry juice
    2 tablespoons cider vinegar
    2 teaspoons soy sauce
    1 pound fully cooked kielbasa *or* Polish
       sausage, cut into 1-1/2-inch pieces
    2 medium tart apples, cut into wedges
    1 medium sweet red pepper, cut into 1-inch
       pieces
    1 medium green pepper, cut into 1-inch
       pieces

In a saucepan, combine sugar and cornstarch. Stir in cranberry juice, vinegar and soy sauce. Bring to a boil; cook and stir for 1-2 minutes or until thickened.

On metal or soaked wooden skewers, alternately thread sausage, apples and peppers. Grill, uncovered, over indirect heat for 8 minutes or until heated through, turning and brushing with glaze occasionally. **Yield:** 8 servings.

Nutritional Analysis: One serving (prepared with reduced-fat turkey sausage) equals 168 calories, 6 g fat (2 g saturated fat), 47 mg cholesterol, 455 mg sodium, 19 g carbohydrate, 2 g fiber, 10 g protein. **Diabetic Exchanges:** 1 meat, 1 vegetable, 1 fruit.

Tangy Ham Steak

(Pictured at right)

Sue Gronholz, Columbus, Wisconsin

This glazed ham steak is a yummy, quick-and-easy main dish. It tastes especially good heated on the grill but works well in the oven broiler, too. On summer weekends back home, Dad does the grilling while Mom prepares the rest of the meal.

    1/3 cup spicy brown mustard
    1/4 cup honey
    1/2 teaspoon grated orange peel
      1 fully cooked ham steak (about 2 pounds)

In a small bowl, combine mustard, honey and orange peel. Brush over one side of ham. Grill, uncovered, over medium-hot heat for 7 minutes. Turn; brush with mustard mixture. Cook until well glazed and heated through, about 7 minutes. **Yield:** 6-8 servings.

Grilled Rosemary Pork Roast

(Pictured on page 50)

Christine Wilson, Sellersville, Pennsylvania

When the family's coming or we're expecting guests for dinner, I often serve this flavorful grilled pork roast —and it's always a winner! Chopped apple and sweet honey complement the rosemary and garlic.

✓ Uses less fat, sugar or salt. Includes Nutritional Analysis and Diabetic Exchanges.

    3 medium tart apples, peeled and chopped
    1 cup unsweetened apple cider *or* juice
    3 green onions, chopped
    3 tablespoons honey
    1 to 2 tablespoons minced fresh rosemary
      or 1 to 2 teaspoons dried rosemary,
      crushed
    2 garlic cloves, minced
    1 boneless pork loin roast (3 pounds)

In a saucepan, combine the first six ingredients; bring to a boil. Reduce heat; simmer, uncovered, for 5 minutes. Cool slightly. Place pork roast in a large resealable plastic bag; add half of the marinade. Seal bag and refrigerate overnight, turning occasionally. Transfer the remaining marinade to a bowl; cover and refrigerate.

Drain and discard marinade. Grill roast, covered, over indirect medium-low heat for 1-1/2 to 2 hours or until a meat thermometer reads 160°, turning occasionally. Let stand for 10 minutes before slicing. Heat reserved marinade; serve with pork. **Yield:** 8 servings.

Nutritional Analysis: One serving equals 312 calories, 9 g fat (3 g saturated fat), 94 mg cholesterol, 79 mg sodium, 19 g carbohydrate, 2 g fiber, 37 g protein. **Diabetic Exchanges:** 3-1/2 lean meat, 1 starch, 1 fat.

Grilled Pork and Poblano Peppers

(Pictured below)

Donna Gay Harris, Springdale, Arkansas

My husband and I entertain a lot in summer, and this has quickly become the most-requested dish. I usually serve it with Mexican rice and a tossed salad.

 4 large poblano peppers
 2 cups (8 ounces) shredded Monterey Jack
   cheese
4-1/2 teaspoons chili powder
1-1/2 teaspoons onion powder
1-1/2 teaspoons ground cumin
 1/2 teaspoon garlic powder
 1/4 teaspoon salt
 1/8 teaspoon aniseed, ground
 1/8 teaspoon cayenne pepper
 2 pork tenderloins (about 1 pound *each*)

Cut the top off each pepper and set the tops aside. Remove the seeds. Stuff the peppers with cheese. Replace the tops and secure with toothpicks; set aside.

 Combine the seasonings; rub over the pork. Grill, covered, over medium-hot heat for 18 minutes or until a meat thermometer reads 160°-170° and juices run clear. Place peppers on sides of grill (not directly over coals); heat for 10 minutes or until browned. **Yield:** 6-8 servings.

Editor's Note: When cutting or seeding hot peppers, use rubber or plastic gloves to protect your hands. Avoid touching your face.

Pork and Apple Skewers

(Pictured above)

Cheryl Plainte, Minot, North Dakota

Necessity was the "mother" of this recipe! I'd already marinated the pork before realizing we were short on kabob vegetables. In place of them, I used apples I had on hand. This has since become one of my most-requested dishes.

 3/4 cup barbecue sauce
 1/2 cup pineapple juice
 1/4 cup honey mustard*
 1/4 cup packed brown sugar
 2 tablespoons soy sauce
 2 tablespoons olive *or* vegetable oil

1-1/2 pounds pork tenderloin, cut into 3/4-inch cubes
5 medium unpeeled tart apples

In a large resealable plastic bag or shallow glass container, combine the first six ingredients; mix well. Reserve 1/2 cup for basting and refrigerate. Add pork to remaining marinade and turn to coat. Seal bag or cover container; refrigerate for at least 1 hour.

Drain and discard marinade. Cut the apples into 1-1/2-in. cubes. Alternate pork and apples on metal or soaked wooden skewers. Grill, uncovered, over medium heat for 3 minutes on each side. Baste with the reserved marinade. Continue turning and basting for 8-10 minutes or until meat juices run clear and apples are tender. **Yield:** 6 servings.

*Editor's Note: As a substitute for honey mustard, combine 2 tablespoons Dijon mustard and 2 tablespoons honey.

Pork Fajita Salad

(Pictured below)

Iola Egle, McCook, Nebraska

For a refreshing take on fajitas, try this savory salad. Your crowd will love the festive layers and creamy guacamole.

1/4 cup olive *or* vegetable oil
2 tablespoons lime juice
1 teaspoon dried oregano
1 teaspoon chili powder
4 boneless pork loin chops (1 inch thick, about 1-1/2 pounds)
2-1/4 cups chicken broth
1 cup uncooked long grain rice
2 ripe avocados, peeled
1 tablespoon lemon juice
1 medium tomato, seeded and chopped
1 jalapeno pepper, seeded and chopped*
2 tablespoons minced fresh cilantro *or* parsley
1 tablespoon finely chopped onion
1 head iceberg lettuce, shredded
1 can (15 ounces) black beans, rinsed and drained
1 cup (4 ounces) shredded sharp cheddar cheese
1 jar (11 ounces) salsa
2 cups (16 ounces) sour cream
Sliced ripe olives and green onions

In a large resealable plastic bag, combine the first four ingredients. Add pork chops. Seal and turn to coat; refrigerate overnight, turning occasionally. Drain, discarding marinade. Grill chops, uncovered, over medium heat for 12-14 minutes or until meat juices run clear, turning once. Thinly slice pork; set aside.

In a saucepan, bring broth to a boil; stir in rice. Return to a boil. Reduce heat; cover and simmer for 15 minutes or until rice is tender. Cool.

Meanwhile, for guacamole, mash avocados with lemon juice. Stir in the tomato, jalapeno, cilantro and onion. In a 5-qt. glass salad bowl, layer the lettuce, beans, cheese, pork and guacamole. Spread with salsa. Combine the rice and sour cream; spread over the salsa. Garnish with olives and green onions. **Yield:** 6 servings.

*Editor's Note: When cutting or seeding hot peppers, use rubber or plastic gloves to protect your hands. Avoid touching your face.

Soaking Skewers

TO HELP prevent wooden skewers from burning or splintering while grilling, soak them in water for 15-30 minutes. Remove them from the water and then thread on the ingredients of your choice.

Stuffed Pork Burgers

(Pictured above)

Jean Smith, Monona, Iowa

I like to prepare pork often and in a variety of ways. Everyone who samples these burgers agrees they are the best! They're a nice alternative to the more-common ground beef burgers.

- 1/2 cup chopped fresh mushrooms
- 1/4 cup sliced green onions
- 1/4 teaspoon garlic powder
- 1 tablespoon butter *or* margarine
- 1-1/2 pounds ground pork
- 2 tablespoons Worcestershire sauce
- 1 teaspoon ground mustard
- 1/2 teaspoon salt
- 1/2 teaspoon pepper
- 4 kaiser rolls, split
- 4 lettuce leaves
- 4 slices red onion
- 8 thin slices tomato

Prepared mustard

In a skillet, saute mushrooms and onions with garlic powder in butter until vegetables are tender. Remove from the heat. In a bowl, combine pork, Worcestershire sauce, mustard, salt and pepper. Shape into eight patties. Spoon mushroom mixture into the center of four patties to within 1/2 in. of edges. Top with remaining patties; pinch edges to seal.

Grill, uncovered, over medium heat for 10-15 minutes, turning once, or until meat juices run clear. Serve on rolls with lettuce, onion, tomato and mustard. **Yield:** 4 servings.

Favorite Pork Chops

(Pictured below)

Alice Hermes, Glen Ullin, North Dakota

As pork raisers, we've served pork many different ways, and this is our absolute favorite. One of our daughters went to state competition in 4-H when she entered these tangy pork chops seasoned with soy sauce, ginger and garlic.

- 1 cup soy sauce
- 1/4 cup diced green pepper
- 1/4 cup packed brown sugar
- 4 teaspoons chopped onion
- 1/2 teaspoon ground ginger
- 2 garlic cloves, minced
- 4 pork loin chops (1 inch thick)
- 2 teaspoons sugar
- 2 teaspoons cornstarch
- 1/2 cup water

In a blender or food processor, combine the soy sauce, green pepper, brown sugar, onion, ginger and garlic; cover and process until smooth. Set aside 2 tablespoons for sauce. Pour the remaining marinade into a large resealable plastic bag or shallow glass container. Add pork chops and turn to coat. Seal or cover and refrigerate for 8 hours or overnight.

Drain and discard the marinade. Grill the pork chops, covered, over medium-hot heat for 5-8 min-

utes on each side or until a meat thermometer reads 160°-170°.

In a saucepan, combine sugar, cornstarch, water and reserved soy sauce mixture; stir until smooth. Bring to a boil; cook and stir for 2 minutes or until thickened. Serve over chops. **Yield:** 4 servings.

Apricot Sausage Kabobs

Susie Lindquist, Ellijay, Georgia

Basted with a simple sweet-sour sauce, these tasty kabobs make a quick meal that's elegant enough for company.

  3/4 cup apricot preserves
  3/4 cup Dijon mustard
    1 pound fully cooked kielbasa *or* Polish
      sausage, cut into 12 pieces
   12 dried apricots
   12 medium fresh mushrooms
Hot cooked rice

In a small bowl, combine preserves and mustard; mix well. Remove 1/2 cup for serving; set aside. Alternate sausage, apricots and mushrooms on four metal or soaked wooden skewers. Grill, covered, over indirect medium heat for 15-20 minutes or until meat

juices run clear. Turn frequently and baste with remaining apricot sauce. Warm the reserved sauce; serve with kabobs and rice. **Yield:** 4 servings.

Glazed Country Ribs

(Pictured at left)

Tamrah Bird, Gaines, Michigan

When I take these mouth-watering ribs to our frequent potlucks at work, they're a hit. I like them basted only with the mildly sweet glaze, but you can serve your favorite barbecue sauce on the side, too. They taste as good reheated as they do right off the grill.

    3 pounds boneless country-style ribs
  3/4 cup pineapple juice
  1/2 cup vegetable oil
  1/2 cup white wine *or* chicken broth
  1/4 cup packed brown sugar
    1 tablespoon Worcestershire sauce
    6 garlic cloves, minced
    1 teaspoon salt
    1 teaspoon pepper
    1 teaspoon dried rosemary, crushed

Place the ribs in a large shallow glass container. Pierce several times with a fork. In a bowl, combine all of the remaining ingredients; set aside 1/2 cup for basting. Pour the remaining marinade over the ribs. Cover and refrigerate for 8 hours or overnight, turning once.

Drain and discard marinade. Grill ribs, covered, over indirect medium heat for 10 minutes on each side. Baste with some of the reserved marinade. Grill 20-25 minutes longer or until meat juices run clear and meat is tender, turning and basting occasionally. **Yield:** 6 servings.

Cleanup Tip

DON'T WASTE TIME scrubbing your grill rack. Instead, put it in a clean plastic bag and spray generously with oven cleaner. Tightly close the bag and leave it overnight. The next day, washing the grate is a breeze.

Barbecued Sage Spareribs

(Pictured below)

Linda Caray, Fruitland, Idaho

Folks love to see a huge platter of these tender barbecued ribs arrive at the table. Since the ribs are cooked ahead, they simply need to be browned and reheated on the grill. I love the easy last-minute preparation and magnificent results. Raves begin with the first bite.

>   6 pounds country-style pork spareribs
>   1 medium onion, chopped
>   2 to 3 garlic cloves, minced
>   2 tablespoons mixed pickling spices
>   1 tablespoon minced fresh sage *or* 1
>   teaspoon rubbed sage
>   1/2 teaspoon hot pepper sauce
>   1 bottle (18 ounces) barbecue sauce

Place ribs in a Dutch oven and cover with water. Add the onion, garlic, pickling spices, sage and hot pepper sauce. Bring to a boil; reduce heat. Cover and simmer for 1-1/2 hours or until tender. Cool slightly; rinse ribs with water to remove spices.

Pour barbecue sauce into a large resealable plastic bag or shallow baking dish. Add ribs; cover and refrigerate overnight. Bring to room temperature. Drain, reserving marinade. Grill ribs, uncovered, over medium heat, turning several times until browned and heated through, about 10 minutes. Place marinade

in a saucepan; bring to a boil, stirring constantly. Brush over the ribs. **Yield:** 6 servings.

Pork with Watermelon Salsa

(Pictured above)

A colorful combination of watermelon, strawberries, kiwifruit and peaches makes a sweet salsa that's ideal to serve alongside grilled pork basted with peach preserves.

>   1 cup seeded chopped watermelon
>   1/2 cup chopped strawberries
>   1/2 cup chopped kiwifruit
>   1/4 cup chopped peaches
>   3 tablespoons lime juice
>   4 teaspoons honey
>   1/2 teaspoon grated lime peel
>   1 to 2 mint leaves, chopped
>   1/2 cup peach preserves
>   3 pork tenderloins (3/4 pound *each*)

For salsa, combine the first eight ingredients in a bowl; set aside. In a saucepan or microwave, heat the preserves for 1 minute. Grill pork, covered, over indirect medium heat for 5 minutes. Turn; brush with some of the preserves. Grill 8-9 minutes longer or until meat

juices run clear and a meat thermometer reads 160°, basting occasionally with preserves. Serve with salsa. **Yield:** 6-8 servings (1-1/4 cups salsa).

Teriyaki Pork Tenderloin

(Pictured below)

Debora Brown, St. Leonard, Maryland

I'm always looking for easy recipes, and this one fits the bill perfectly. I've made this pork several times for company and received many compliments on it.

- 1/2 cup soy sauce
- 1/4 cup olive *or* vegetable oil
- 4 teaspoons brown sugar
- 2 teaspoons ground ginger
- 1 teaspoon pepper
- 2 garlic cloves, minced
- 4 pork tenderloins (3/4 to 1 pound *each*)
Coarsely ground pepper, optional

In a large resealable plastic bag, combine the first six ingredients; add pork. Seal bag and turn to coat; refrigerate for 4 hours, turning occasionally.

Drain and discard marinade. Grill the tenderloin, covered, over indirect medium heat for 8-9 minutes on each side or until meat juices run clear and a meat thermometer reads 160°. Sprinkle with pepper if desired. **Yield:** 8 servings.

Oriental Pork Chops

Annie Arnold, Plymouth, Minnesota

I experimented with a poultry marinade until I came up with this nicely seasoned version for pork chops.

☑ Uses less fat, sugar or salt. Includes Nutritional Analysis and Diabetic Exchanges.

- 3 tablespoons soy sauce
- 3 tablespoons honey
- 1 tablespoon lemon juice
- 1 tablespoon olive *or* vegetable oil
- 3 garlic cloves, minced
- 1/2 teaspoon ground ginger
- 4 boneless pork chops (1/2 to 3/4 inch thick)

In a large resealable plastic bag or shallow glass container, combine the first six ingredients. Add pork and turn to coat. Seal or cover; refrigerate for 4-8 hours. Grill, uncovered, over medium heat for 10-12 minutes or until juices run clear, turning once. **Yield:** 4 servings.

Nutritional Analysis: One serving (prepared with reduced-sodium soy sauce) equals 225 calories, 420 mg sodium, 55 mg cholesterol, 16 gm carbohydrate, 21 gm protein, 9 gm fat. **Diabetic Exchanges:** 3 lean meat, 2 starch.

Pork Burgers Deluxe

Peggy Bellar, Howard, Kansas

I found this recipe in a book I got for my wedding. The flavor of the burgers is fantastic.

- 1/3 cup vinegar
- 1/4 cup packed brown sugar
- 1 small onion, chopped
- 2 tablespoons soy sauce
- 1 teaspoon salt
- 1 teaspoon garlic salt
- 2 pounds ground pork
- 1 can (20 ounces) pineapple slices, drained
- 10 bacon strips
- 10 hamburger buns, split

Combine the first six ingredients; add pork and mix well. Shape into 10 patties. Top each with a pineapple slice; wrap with a bacon strip and secure with a toothpick. Grill over medium-hot heat for 15-20 minutes or until meat juices run clear, turning once. Serve on buns. **Yield:** 10 servings.

Tropical Sausage Kabobs

Joan Hallford, North Richland Hills, Texas

I've prepared these yummy kabobs for family and friends for years. They're a favorite.

>   1 tablespoon cornstarch
>   3 tablespoons Dijon mustard
> 3/4 cup ginger ale
> 1/3 cup honey
>   1 pound fully cooked kielbasa *or* Polish sausage, cut into 1-inch chunks
>   4 medium firm bananas, cut into 1-inch slices
>   2 fresh pineapples, peeled and cut into 1-inch chunks *or* 2 cans (20 ounces *each*) pineapple chunks, drained

In a small saucepan, combine the cornstarch and mustard until smooth. Gradually stir in ginger ale and honey until well blended. Bring to a boil; cook and stir for 2 minutes or until thickened and bubbly.

Alternately thread sausage and fruit onto metal or soaked wooden skewers. Brush with mustard sauce. Grill, uncovered, over medium-hot heat for 4 minutes or until evenly browned, basting and turning several times. **Yield:** 4-6 servings.

Honey Barbecued Ribs

(Pictured above)

Joyce Duff, Mansfield, Ohio

My family celebrates four birthdays in July, and these tender ribs are a must at our joint get-together. Honey adds wonderful flavor to the homemade sauce.

>   3 pounds country-style pork ribs
> 1/2 teaspoon garlic salt
> 1/2 teaspoon pepper
>   1 cup ketchup
> 1/2 cup packed brown sugar
> 1/2 cup honey
> 1/4 cup spicy brown mustard
>   2 tablespoons Worcestershire sauce
> 1-1/2 teaspoons liquid smoke, optional

Place ribs in a large kettle or Dutch oven; sprinkle with garlic salt and pepper. Add enough water to cover; bring to a boil. Reduce heat; cover and simmer for 1 hour or until juices run clear and ribs are tender; drain.

Meanwhile, combine the remaining ingredients. Grill ribs, uncovered, over medium heat for 10-12 minutes, basting with sauce and turning occasionally. **Yield:** 4 servings.

Marinated Ham Steaks

Maribeth Edwards, Follansbee, West Virginia

It's a snap to combine this zippy marinade...and you can vary the marinating time to fit your day's activities.

> 1-1/2 cups pineapple juice
>   1/4 cup packed brown sugar
>   2 tablespoons butter *or* margarine, melted
>   1 to 2 tablespoons ground mustard
>   1 garlic clove, minced
>   1/4 teaspoon paprika
>   2 fully cooked ham steaks (1 pound *each*)

In a large resealable plastic bag or shallow glass container, combine the first six ingredients; mix well. Add ham and turn to coat. Seal or cover; refrigerate for at least 2 hours, turning occasionally.

Drain and reserve marinade. Place the marinade in a saucepan; bring to a rolling boil. Grill ham, uncovered, over medium-hot heat for 3-4 minutes on each side, basting frequently with marinade. **Yield:** 6 servings.

Tummy Dogs

(Pictured below)

Myra Innes, Auburn, Kansas

Looking for a fun and flavorful way to jazz up hot dogs? Try these bacon-wrapped versions with zippy Dijon mustard. They don't take long to fix. And your tummy will thank you.

      8 bacon strips
      8 hot dogs
      4 ounces Monterey Jack cheese, cut into
         strips
  1/4 cup butter *or* margarine, softened
  1/4 cup Dijon mustard
      8 hot dog buns
      1 small onion, thinly sliced, optional
      1 can (4 ounces) diced green chilies, optional

Partially cook bacon; drain on paper towels. Cut a 1/4-in. lengthwise slit in each hot dog; place cheese in each slit. Starting at one end, wrap bacon in a spiral around hot dog; secure with toothpicks. Split buns just halfway. Combine butter and mustard; spread inside buns. Set aside.

On a covered grill over medium heat, cook hot dogs with cheese side down for 2 minutes. Turn and grill 3-4 minutes longer or until bacon is crisp and cheese is melted. Place buns on grill with cut side down; grill until lightly toasted. Remove toothpicks from the hot dogs; serve in buns with onion and chilies if desired. **Yield:** 8 sandwiches.

Ribs with Plum Sauce

(Pictured above)

Marie Hoyer, Hodgenville, Kentucky

I found the recipe for this tangy-sweet basting sauce when a surplus of plums sent me searching for new ideas to use all the fruit. In summer, I like to finish the ribs on the grill, brushing on the sauce, after first baking them in the oven.

  5 to 6 pounds pork spareribs
  3/4 cup soy sauce
  3/4 cup plum jam *or* apricot preserves
  3/4 cup honey
  2 to 3 garlic cloves, minced

Cut ribs into serving-size pieces; place with bone side down on a rack in a shallow roasting pan. Cover and bake at 350° for 1 hour or until ribs are tender; drain. Combine remaining ingredients; brush some of the sauce over ribs. Grill over medium heat, uncovered, for 30 minutes, brushing occasionally with sauce. **Yield:** 6 servings.

Basting Basics

BRUSH ON thick or sweet sauces during the last 10-15 minutes of cooking, basting and turning every few minutes to prevent burning.

Use tongs to turn meat instead of a meat fork to avoid piercing and losing juices.

Smoked Tenderloin Salad

(Pictured below)

Roberta Whitesell, Phoenix, Arizona

During our hot summers, I rely on salads. In this recipe, the pork is grilled so I can stay out of the kitchen.

 Uses less fat, sugar or salt. Includes Nutritional Analysis and Diabetic Exchanges.

DRESSING:
- 1/2 cup orange juice
- 2 tablespoons olive *or* vegetable oil
- 2 tablespoons cider vinegar
- 1 tablespoon grated orange peel
- 2 teaspoons honey
- 2 teaspoons Dijon mustard
- 1/2 teaspoon coarsely ground pepper

SALAD:
- 1 pork tenderloin (1 pound), trimmed
- 10 cups torn salad greens
- 2 seedless oranges, peeled and sliced
- 1/4 cup chopped pistachios *or* cashews, optional

In a small bowl, combine all dressing ingredients; cover and chill. Grill pork, covered, over medium heat for 15-20 minutes or until a meat thermometer reads 160°-170°, turning occasionally. Let stand for 5 minutes; thinly slice tenderloin.

To serve, line large platter with greens; top with orange sections and tenderloin. Sprinkle with nuts if desired. Drizzle with dressing. **Yield:** 5 servings.

Nutritional Analysis: One serving (prepared without nuts) equals 223 calories, 99 mg sodium, 54 mg cholesterol, 14 gm carbohydrate, 21 gm protein, 9 gm fat. **Diabetic Exchanges:** 2-1/2 lean meat, 1 vegetable, 1/2 fruit, 1/2 fat.

Zesty Grilled Chops

(Pictured above)

Bernice Germann, Napoleon, Ohio

My sister gave me the recipe for this easy five-ingredient marinade. It keeps the meat so moist and tasty…now this is the only way my husband wants his pork chops prepared.

- 3/4 cup soy sauce
- 1/4 cup lemon juice
- 1 tablespoon chili sauce
- 1 tablespoon brown sugar
- 1/4 teaspoon garlic powder
- 6 rib *or* loin pork chops (3/4 inch thick)

In a large resealable plastic bag or shallow glass container, combine the first five ingredients; mix well. Remove 1/4 cup for basting and refrigerate. Add pork chops to remaining marinade; turn to coat. Cover and refrigerate for 3 hours or overnight, turning once.

Drain chops, discarding marinade. Grill, covered, over medium-hot heat for 4 minutes. Turn; baste with reserved marinade. Grill 4-7 minutes longer or until juices run clear. **Yield:** 6 servings.

Mandarin Pork

(Pictured below)

Flo Weiss, Seaside, Oregon

I often serve this pork with fried rice and Chinese-style vegetables. It also makes a great appetizer by itself. Folks have fun dipping the nuggets into the two home-made sauces.

      1 cup soy sauce
  1/2 cup vegetable oil
      3 tablespoons honey
      1 tablespoon ground ginger
      1 tablespoon ground mustard
      1 garlic clove, minced
      2 pork tenderloins (3/4 to 1 pound *each*)
SWEET-AND-SOUR SAUCE:
  1/2 cup orange marmalade
      2 tablespoons vinegar
      1 tablespoon diced pimientos
  1/8 teaspoon paprika
Dash salt
FIRE-HOT MUSTARD:
  1/4 cup boiling water
  1/4 cup ground mustard
  1/2 teaspoon salt

Combine the first six ingredients in a large resealable plastic bag or shallow glass container; add

pork and turn to coat. Seal bag or cover container; refrigerate overnight, turning meat several times.

Meanwhile, combine sauce ingredients in a bowl; cover and chill. In another bowl, stir boiling water into mustard; add salt and stir until smooth. Cover and let stand at room temperature for 1 hour; chill.

Drain meat and discard marinade. Grill, covered, over medium heat, turning occasionally, for 18-20 minutes or until a meat thermometer reads 160°-170°. Let stand for 5 minutes before slicing. Serve with sauce and mustard for dipping. **Yield:** 6-8 servings.

Carry-Along Hot Dogs

Lorraine Priebe, Noonan, North Dakota

These versatile sandwiches can be made over the grill or in the oven, so they're great any time of year. We especially like them when camping.

  1/3 cup ketchup
      2 tablespoons sweet pickle relish
      1 tablespoon finely chopped onion
      1 teaspoon prepared mustard
      8 hot dog buns, split
      8 slices American cheese
      8 hot dogs

In a small bowl, combine the first four ingredients. Place a slice of cheese on the bottom half of each bun. Slice hot dogs in half lengthwise; place two halves on each bun. Spoon 1 tablespoon of sauce over each hot dog. Replace top of bun and wrap each sandwich in foil.

Grill, uncovered, over medium heat, turning often, for 10-15 minutes; or place on a baking sheet and bake at 350° for 10 minutes. **Yield:** 8 servings.

Pork Pointers

WHEN BUYING PORK, look for meat that's pale pink with a small amount of marbling and white fat. The darker pink the flesh, the older the animal.

The best way to test pork's doneness is with a meat thermometer. The internal temperature should read 160°-170°. Cutting it to see if it's still pink lets too many juices out.

Bratwurst Supper

(Pictured above)

Janice Meyer, Medford, Wisconsin

This meal-in-one grills to perfection in a heavy-duty foil bag and is ideal for camping. Loaded with chunks of bratwurst, red potatoes, mushrooms and carrots, it's easy to season with onion soup mix, a little soy sauce and pepper.

 3 pounds uncooked bratwurst links
 3 pounds small red potatoes, cut into wedges
 1 pound baby carrots
 1 large red onion, sliced and separated into
  rings
 2 jars (4-1/2 ounces *each*) whole mushrooms,
  drained
1/4 cup butter *or* margarine, cubed
 1 envelope onion soup mix
 2 tablespoons soy sauce
1/2 teaspoon pepper

Cut bratwurst links into thirds. Place the bratwurst, potatoes, carrots, onion and mushrooms in a heavy-duty foil bag (17 in. x 15 in.). Dot with butter. Sprinkle with soup mix, soy sauce and pepper. Seal tightly; turn to coat.

 Grill, covered, over medium heat for 45-55 min-

utes or until vegetables are tender and sausage is no longer pink, turning once. **Yield:** 12 servings.

Country Pork Ribs

(Pictured below)

Brian Johnson, LaGrange, Georgia

These hearty ribs feature a lip-smacking sauce that's deliciously tangy with just the right hint of sweetness. The marinade is absolutely terrific for country-style ribs, but I've found it's great with other meats, too.

 1 cup grapefruit *or* orange juice
 1 cup ketchup
1/2 cup cider vinegar
1/4 cup soy sauce
1/4 cup Worcestershire sauce
 2 tablespoons prepared horseradish
 2 tablespoons prepared mustard
 2 teaspoons ground ginger
 1 to 2 teaspoons hot pepper sauce
1/2 teaspoon garlic powder
 4 to 5 pounds country-style pork ribs
1/4 cup honey
 2 tablespoons brown sugar

In a bowl, combine the first 10 ingredients; mix well. Pour 1-1/2 cups marinade into a large resealable

plastic bag; add the ribs. Seal and turn to coat; refrigerate for at least 4 hours. Cover and refrigerate remaining marinade.

Drain and discard marinade from the ribs. Grill, covered, over indirect medium heat for 20 minutes on each side. Meanwhile, in a saucepan, combine the honey, brown sugar and reserved marinade. Bring to a boil; cook and stir for 2 minutes or until slightly thickened.

Baste ribs with some of the sauce. Grill 15-20 minutes longer or until a meat thermometer reads 160°, turning and basting occasionally. Serve with the remaining sauce. **Yield:** 8 servings.

Corn-Stuffed Pork Chops

(Pictured above)

Elizabeth Jussaume, Lowell, Massachusetts

For an eye-catching entree, I grill pork chops filled with a colorful corn, pimiento and green pepper stuffing.

 Uses less fat, sugar or salt. Includes Nutritional Analysis and Diabetic Exchanges.

    6 bone-in center loin pork chops (1 inch thick,
      about 10 ounces *each*)
  3/4 teaspoon salt, *divided*
  1/4 teaspoon pepper, *divided*
  1/4 cup chopped green pepper

  1/4 cup chopped onion
    1 tablespoon butter *or* stick margarine
1-1/2 cups bread cubes, toasted
  1/2 cup frozen corn, thawed
  1/4 cup egg substitute
    2 tablespoons chopped pimientos
  1/4 teaspoon ground cumin

Cut a pocket in each pork chop; sprinkle 1/4 teaspoon salt and 1/8 teaspoon pepper in pockets. Set aside. In a nonstick skillet, saute green pepper and onion in butter until tender. Transfer to a bowl.

Add the bread cubes, corn, egg substitute, pimientos, cumin and remaining salt and pepper; mix well. Stuff into pork chops; secure with wooden toothpicks.

Before starting the grill, coat grill rack with nonstick cooking spray. Grill chops, covered, over medium indirect heat for 15-18 minutes on each side or until a meat thermometer inserted in stuffing reads 160°. **Yield:** 6 servings.

Nutritional Analysis: One serving (1 stuffed pork chop) equals 308 calories, 12 g fat (5 g saturated fat), 102 mg cholesterol, 458 mg sodium, 10 g carbohydrate, 1 g fiber, 38 g protein. **Diabetic Exchanges:** 5 lean meat, 1/2 starch.

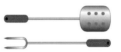

Reuben Burgers

Jeanne Fenstermaker, Kendallville, Indiana

I use ground pork and sauerkraut in this fun alternative to traditional burgers. For true Reuben flavor, put the ketchup away and top things off with Thousand Island salad dressing.

    2 pounds ground pork
    2 teaspoons salt
    1 teaspoon pepper
    1 garlic clove, minced
  1/2 cup sauerkraut, drained
    8 slices Swiss cheese
    8 hamburger buns, split and toasted

In a bowl, combine pork, salt, pepper and garlic; mix well. Shape into 16 patties, about 3/8 in. thick. Spoon 1 tablespoon sauerkraut in the center of eight patties; top each with a second patty and press edges to seal.

Grill, uncovered, over medium heat for 6-8 minutes on each side or until juices run clear. Top with cheese. Serve on buns. **Yield:** 8 servings.

Fish and Seafood

Lemon Grilled Salmon (p. 74)

Chapter 4

Shrimp Kabobs

(Pictured above)

Cheryl Williams, Evington, Virginia

My family always asks me to prepare these tangy and juicy kabobs during our beach getaways.

✓ Uses less fat, sugar or salt. Includes Nutritional Analysis and Diabetic Exchanges.

    1 can (8 ounces) tomato sauce
    1 cup chopped onion
  1/2 cup water
  1/4 cup packed brown sugar
  1/4 cup lemon juice
    3 tablespoons Worcestershire sauce
    2 tablespoons canola oil
    2 tablespoons prepared mustard
  1/2 teaspoon salt
  1/2 teaspoon pepper
    1 can (20 ounces) unsweetened pineapple
      chunks
    1 pound uncooked medium shrimp, peeled
      and deveined (about 32)
    1 medium green pepper, cut into chunks
    1 medium onion, cut into chunks
    3 cups hot cooked rice

In a saucepan, combine the first 10 ingredients. Bring to a boil. Reduce heat; simmer, uncovered, for 15 minutes.

Drain pineapple, reserving 2 tablespoons juice (save remaining juice for another use); set pineapple aside. Stir reserved juice into sauce. Pour half into a bowl for basting; cover and refrigerate. Pour remaining sauce into a large resealable plastic bag; add shrimp. Seal bag and turn to coat; refrigerate for 2-3 hours.

Drain and discard marinade. Alternately thread shrimp, pineapple, green pepper and onion on eight metal or soaked wooden skewers.

Coat grill rack with nonstick cooking spray before starting the grill. Grill kabobs, covered, over medium heat for 5 minutes on each side or until shrimp turn pink, basting occasionally with reserved sauce. Serve over rice. **Yield:** 4 servings.

Nutritional Analysis: One serving (2 kabobs with 3/4 cup rice) equals 428 calories, 6 g fat (1 g saturated fat), 161 mg cholesterol, 775 mg sodium, 71 g carbohydrate, 4 g fiber, 23 g protein. **Diabetic Exchanges:** 3 lean meat, 2-1/2 starch, 2 vegetable, 1 fruit, 1 fat.

Barbecued Alaskan Salmon

(Pictured below)

Janis Smoke, King Salmon, Alaska

We eat salmon all summer long, and this is our favorite way to fix it. The mild sauce—brushed on as the fish grills—really enhances the taste.

2 tablespoons butter *or* margarine
2 tablespoons brown sugar
1 to 2 garlic cloves, minced
1 tablespoon lemon juice
2 teaspoons soy sauce
1/2 teaspoon pepper
4 salmon steaks (1 inch thick)

In a small saucepan, combine the first six ingredients. Cook and stir until sugar is dissolved. Meanwhile, grill salmon, covered, over medium-hot heat for 5 minutes. Turn salmon; baste with the butter sauce. Grill 7-9 minutes longer, turning and basting occasionally, or until the salmon flakes easily with a fork. **Yield:** 4 servings.

Crispy Catfish

(Pictured above right)

Rhonda Dietz, Garden City, Kansas

Grilling is my family's favorite way to fix meals. Because my husband savors well-prepared foods, this recipe quickly became one of his most requested.

3/4 cup finely crushed saltines (22 crackers)
1 teaspoon seasoned salt
1/2 teaspoon celery salt
1/2 teaspoon garlic salt
4 catfish fillets (about 8 ounces *each*)
1/3 cup butter *or* margarine, melted

In a shallow dish, combine the first four ingredients. Pat fillets dry; dip in butter, then coat with crumb mixture. Coat grill rack with nonstick cooking spray before starting grill. Grill fillets, covered, over medium-hot heat for 10 minutes or until fish flakes easily with a fork, carefully turning once. **Yield:** 4 servings.

Flavorful Flounder

Tammy Sanborn, Alto, Michigan

When my grandparents lived in the Florida Keys, Grandpop went fishing every day. They ate fish often, so

Grandmom had to find creative ways to serve it. The Parmesan cheese in this fast recipe adds just the right flavor to the flounder.

2 pounds flounder *or* sole fillets
2 tablespoons lemon juice
1/2 cup grated Parmesan cheese
1/4 cup butter *or* margarine, melted
3 tablespoons mayonnaise
3 tablespoons chopped green onions
1/4 teaspoon salt

Coat a piece of heavy-duty foil (about 14 in. x 14 in.) with nonstick cooking spray. Place fillets on foil; brush with lemon juice. Crimp foil, forming edges. Place foil flat on the grill (do not seal).

Grill, covered, over medium-hot heat for 4 minutes. Combine Parmesan cheese, butter, mayonnaise, onions and salt; brush over the fillets. Grill 3-4 minutes longer or until fish flakes easily with a fork. **Yield:** 4-6 servings.

Fish Won't Stick

TO KEEP grilled fish from sticking, brush the grill rack lightly with vegetable oil or spray with nonstick cooking spray before starting the grill. Do the same thing if using a fish basket for grilling.

Lemon Grilled Salmon

(Pictured below and on page 70)

Lisa Kivirist, Browntown, Wisconsin

Mom proudly serves this tender, flaky fish to family and guests. A savory marinade that includes dill gives the salmon mouth-watering flavor. Since it can be grilled or broiled, we enjoy it year-round.

 Uses less fat, sugar or salt. Includes Nutritional Analysis and Diabetic Exchanges.

> 2 teaspoons snipped fresh dill *or* 3/4 teaspoon dill weed
> 1/2 teaspoon lemon-pepper seasoning
> 1/2 teaspoon salt, optional
> 1/4 teaspoon garlic powder
> 1 salmon fillet (1-1/2 pounds)
> 1/4 cup packed brown sugar
> 3 tablespoons chicken broth
> 3 tablespoons vegetable oil
> 3 tablespoons soy sauce
> 3 tablespoons finely chopped green onions
> 1 small lemon, thinly sliced
> 2 onion slices, separated into rings

Sprinkle dill, lemon-pepper, salt if desired and garlic powder over salmon. Place in a large resealable plastic bag or shallow glass container. Combine brown

sugar, broth, oil, soy sauce and green onions; pour over the salmon. Seal or cover and refrigerate for 1 hour, turning once. Drain and discard marinade. Place salmon skin side down on grill over medium heat; arrange lemon and onion slices over the top. Cover and cook for 15-20 minutes or until fish flakes easily with a fork. **Yield:** 6 servings.

Nutritional Analysis: One serving (prepared with salt-free lemon-pepper seasoning and reduced-sodium soy sauce and without salt) equals 199 calories, 181 mg sodium, 68 mg cholesterol, 7 gm carbohydrate, 22 gm protein, 9 gm fat. **Diabetic Exchanges:** 3 lean meat, 1 vegetable.

Editor's Note: Salmon can be broiled instead of grilled. Place the fillet on a greased broiler pan. Broil 3-4 in. from the heat for 6-8 minutes or until fish flakes easily with a fork.

Marinated Catfish Fillets

(Pictured above and on front cover)

Pauletta Boese, Macon, Mississippi

Recently, we hosted a group of young people from Canada. Since we wanted to give them a true taste of the South, this was served. They raved about it.

6 catfish fillets (about 8 ounces *each*)
1 bottle (16 ounces) Italian salad dressing
1 can (10-3/4 ounces) condensed tomato
   soup, undiluted
3/4 cup vegetable oil
3/4 cup sugar
1/3 cup vinegar
3/4 teaspoon celery seed
3/4 teaspoon salt
3/4 teaspoon pepper
3/4 teaspoon ground mustard
1/2 teaspoon garlic powder

Place fillets in a large resealable plastic bag or shallow glass container; cover with salad dressing. Seal bag or cover container; refrigerate for 1 hour, turning occasionally. Drain and discard marinade.

Combine remaining ingredients; mix well. Remove 1 cup for basting. (Refrigerate remaining sauce for another use.)

Grill fillets, covered, over medium-hot heat for 3 minutes on each side. Brush with the basting sauce. Continue grilling for 6-8 minutes or until fish flakes easily with a fork, turning once and basting several times. **Yield:** 6 servings.

Editor's Note: Reserved sauce may be used to brush on grilled or broiled fish, chicken, turkey or pork.

Herbed Orange Roughy

Sue Kroening, Mattoon, Illinois

The simple seasonings in this recipe enhance the pleasant, mild flavor of orange roughy. It's a quick and easy way to prepare fish that my whole family enjoys.

2 tablespoons lemon juice
1 tablespoon butter *or* margarine, melted
1/2 teaspoon dried thyme
1/2 teaspoon grated lemon peel
1/4 teaspoon salt
1/4 teaspoon paprika
1/8 teaspoon garlic powder
4 orange roughy, red snapper, catfish *or*
   trout fillets (6 ounces *each*)

In a shallow glass container, combine the first seven ingredients; dip fillets. Grill, covered, over hot heat for 10 minutes or until fish flakes easily with a fork. **Yield:** 4 servings.

Caesar Salmon Fillets

(Pictured below)

Joan Garneau, Ellenton, Florida

Not only is this my husband's favorite meal, but it's a dish dinner guests enjoy as well.

 Uses less fat, sugar or salt. Includes Nutritional Analysis and Diabetic Exchanges.

4 salmon fillets (6 ounces *each*)
1/2 cup fat-free Caesar salad dressing
1/4 cup reduced-sodium soy sauce
1 garlic clove, minced

Place salmon fillets in a large resealable plastic bag; add the salad dressing. Seal bag and turn to coat; refrigerate for at least 2 hours.

Drain and discard marinade. Coat grill rack with nonstick cooking spray before starting the grill. Place salmon skin side down on grill rack. Grill, covered, over medium heat for 5 minutes. In a small bowl, combine soy sauce and garlic; brush over salmon. Grill 10-15 minutes longer or until fish flakes easily with a fork, basting occasionally. **Yield:** 4 servings.

Nutritional Analysis: One serving (1 fillet) equals 322 calories, 18 g fat (4 g saturated fat), 112 mg cholesterol, 880 mg sodium, 2 g carbohydrate, trace fiber, 35 g protein. **Diabetic Exchange:** 5 lean meat.

Basil-Marinated Fish

(Pictured above)

Our Test Kitchen found that basil vinegar makes a delightfully pleasant marinade for orange roughy or halibut.

BASIL VINEGAR:
    1 cup fresh basil leaves, crushed
    2 cups white wine vinegar
FISH:
  1/4 cup Basil Vinegar (recipe above)
    2 tablespoons olive *or* canola oil
    1 tablespoon *each* chopped fresh basil, thyme, oregano and parsley *or* 1 teaspoon *each* dried basil, thyme, oregano and parsley flakes
    2 garlic cloves, minced
    1 teaspoon grated lemon peel
  1/2 teaspoon salt
  1/4 teaspoon pepper
    2 orange roughy *or* halibut fillets (1 pound)

Place crushed basil leaves in a sterilized pint jar. Heat vinegar just until simmering; pour over basil. Cool to room temperature. Cover and let stand in a cool dark place for 24 hours; strain and discard basil.

In a large resealable plastic bag, combine 1/4 cup basil vinegar, oil, herbs, garlic, lemon peel, salt and pepper. Add fillets; seal bag and turn to coat. Refrigerate for 30 minutes, turning once or twice. Drain and discard marinade.

Coat grill rack with nonstick cooking spray before starting grill. Grill fillets, covered, over medium-hot heat for 7-10 minutes or until fish flakes easily with a fork. **Yield:** 4 servings.

Gingered Honey Salmon

(Pictured below)

Dan Strumberger, Farmington, Minnesota

Ginger, garlic powder and green onion blend nicely in an easy marinade that gives pleasant flavor to salmon. We also like to use this versatile mixture when grilling chicken, but we've found it tastes even better when marinated in the fridge overnight.

  1/3 cup orange juice
  1/3 cup soy sauce
  1/4 cup honey
    1 green onion, chopped
    1 teaspoon ground ginger
    1 teaspoon garlic powder
    1 salmon fillet (1-1/2 pounds and 3/4 inch thick)

Coat grill rack with nonstick cooking spray before starting the grill. In a bowl, combine the first six ingredients; mix well. Set aside 1/3 cup for basting; cover and refrigerate. Pour remaining marinade into a large resealable plastic bag or shallow glass container; add salmon and turn to coat. Seal or cover and refrigerate for 30 minutes, turning once or twice.

Drain and discard marinade. Place salmon skin side down on grill. Grill, covered, over medium-hot heat for 5 minutes. Baste with reserved marinade. Grill 10-15 minutes longer or until fish flakes easily with a fork, basting frequently. **Yield:** 4-6 servings.

Creole Catfish Fillets

Dave Bremstone, Plantation, Florida

I rub catfish fillets with a pleasant mixture of seasonings before cooking them quickly on the grill.

 Uses less fat, sugar or salt. Includes Nutritional Analysis and Diabetic Exchanges.

    3 tablespoons reduced-fat plain yogurt
    2 tablespoons finely chopped onion
    1 tablespoon fat-free mayonnaise
    1 tablespoon Dijon mustard
    1 tablespoon ketchup
  1/2 teaspoon dried thyme
  1/4 teaspoon grated lemon peel
    1 teaspoon paprika
  1/2 teaspoon onion powder
  1/4 teaspoon salt
  1/8 teaspoon cayenne pepper
    4 catfish fillets (4 ounces *each*)
    4 lemon wedges

In a bowl, combine the first seven ingredients. Cover and refrigerate until serving. In another bowl, combine the paprika, onion powder, salt and cayenne; rub over both sides of fillets.

Grill, covered, in a grill basket coated with nonstick cooking spray over medium-hot heat, or broil 6 in. from the heat for 5-6 minutes on each side or until fish flakes easily with a fork. Serve with lemon wedges and yogurt sauce. **Yield:** 4 servings.

Nutritional Analysis: One serving (1 fillet with about 1 tablespoon sauce) equals 182 calories, 9 g fat (2 g saturated fat), 54 mg cholesterol, 382 mg sodium, 5 g carbohydrate, 1 g fiber, 19 g protein. **Diabetic Exchanges:** 3 lean meat, 1/2 fat.

Salmon with Citrus Salsa

(Pictured above right)

Nancy Shirvani, Terryville, Connecticut

This grilled salmon is a surefire winner! It makes a perfect light summer supper.

 Uses less fat, sugar or salt. Includes Nutritional Analysis and Diabetic Exchanges.

  1/2 cup raspberry vinegar
  1/4 cup reduced-sodium soy sauce

    2 tablespoons minced fresh cilantro *or* parsley
1-1/2 teaspoons ground ginger *or* 2 tablespoons minced fresh gingerroot
    1 tablespoon olive *or* canola oil
  1/2 teaspoon hot pepper sauce
  1/8 teaspoon pepper
    4 salmon fillets (6 ounces *each*)
CITRUS SALSA:
  3/4 cup pink grapefruit segments, cut into bite-size pieces
  1/2 cup orange segments, cut into bite-size pieces
    1 tablespoon raspberry vinegar
    1 tablespoon honey
    1 teaspoon minced fresh cilantro *or* parsley
  1/8 teaspoon ground ginger *or* 1 teaspoon minced fresh gingerroot
  1/8 teaspoon hot pepper sauce

In a large resealable plastic bag, combine the first seven ingredients; add salmon. Seal bag and turn to coat; refrigerate for 2 hours. Meanwhile, in a bowl, combine salsa ingredients. Cover and refrigerate.

Drain and discard marinade. Coat grill rack with nonstick cooking spray before starting grill. Place salmon, skin side down, on grill. Grill, covered, over medium heat for 15-20 minutes or until fish flakes easily with a fork. Serve with salsa. **Yield:** 4 servings.

Nutritional Analysis: One serving (1 fillet with 3 tablespoons salsa) equals 361 calories, 19 g fat (4 g saturated fat), 112 mg cholesterol, 241 mg sodium, 12 g carbohydrate, 1 g fiber, 35 g protein. **Diabetic Exchanges:** 4-1/2 lean meat, 1 fruit, 1 fat.

Teriyaki Tuna Steaks

(Pictured below)

Michelle Dennis, Clarks Hill, Indiana

After sampling some wonderful tuna at a Japanese restaurant, I decided to try my hand at coming up with the recipe. It took a little trial and error, but I was pleased with the results—these seasonings are a lovely complement to the tuna.

 Uses less fat, sugar or salt. Includes Nutritional Analysis and Diabetic Exchanges.

    1/4 cup reduced-sodium soy sauce
      3 tablespoons brown sugar
      3 tablespoons olive *or* canola oil
      2 tablespoons white wine vinegar *or* cider
        vinegar
      2 tablespoons sherry *or* chicken broth
      2 tablespoons unsweetened pineapple juice
      2 garlic cloves, minced
1-1/2 teaspoons ground ginger *or* 2 tablespoons
        minced fresh gingerroot
      4 tuna steaks (6 ounces *each*)

In a bowl, combine the first eight ingredients; mix well. Remove 1/3 cup to a small bowl for basting; cover and refrigerate. Pour remaining marinade into a large resealable plastic bag; add tuna. Seal bag and turn to coat; refrigerate for up to 1 hour.

Coat grill rack with nonstick cooking spray before starting the grill. Drain and discard marinade. Grill tuna, uncovered, over medium heat for 5-6 minutes on each side or until fish flakes easily with a fork, basting frequently with reserved marinade. **Yield:** 4 servings.

Nutritional Analysis: One serving equals 338 calories, 9 g fat (1 g saturated fat), 99 mg cholesterol, 484 mg sodium, 9 g carbohydrate, trace fiber, 52 g protein. **Diabetic Exchanges:** 5 lean meat, 1/2 starch.

Tangy Shrimp and Scallops

(Pictured above)

Lauren Llewellyn, Raleigh, North Carolina

Shrimp and scallops together make this a special dish for company. I serve these appealing kabobs over pasta with a green salad and garlic bread.

    28 large shrimp (about 1-1/2 pounds), peeled
        and deveined
    28 sea scallops (about 1/2 pound)
   1/2 cup butter *or* margarine
      7 tablespoons lemon juice
      5 tablespoons Worcestershire sauce
      1 to 2 teaspoons garlic powder
      1 teaspoon paprika

Place shrimp and scallops in a large resealable plastic bag. In a microwave-safe bowl, combine the butter, lemon juice, Worcestershire sauce, garlic powder and paprika. Microwave at 50% power for 1-1/2

minutes or until butter is melted. Stir to blend; set aside 1/3 cup for basting. Pour remaining marinade over shrimp and scallops. Seal bag and turn to coat; refrigerate for 1 hour, turning occasionally.

Drain and discard marinade. Alternately thread shrimp and scallops on metal or soaked wooden skewers. Grill, uncovered, over medium-hot heat for 6 minutes, turning once. Brush with reserved marinade. Grill 8-10 minutes longer or until shrimp turn pink and scallops are opaque. **Yield:** 4 servings.

Orange Roughy Bundles

(Pictured below)

Margaret Wilson, Hemet, California

Cleanup is a breeze with this simple seafood supper. Each meal-in-one packet contains zucchini, red pepper and a flaky full-flavored fish fillet. It cooks in no time and is just as delicious with flounder or sole.

    4 fresh *or* frozen orange roughy fillets
       (6 ounces *each*), thawed
1/4 cup grated Parmesan cheese
1/8 to 1/4 teaspoon cayenne pepper
    2 medium zucchini, cut into 1/4-inch slices
    1 small sweet red pepper, julienned
1/2 teaspoon salt

Place each fillet on a piece of heavy-duty foil (about 12 in. square). Sprinkle with Parmesan cheese and cayenne. Top with zucchini, red pepper and salt. Fold foil over vegetables and seal tightly. Grill, covered, over indirect heat for 8-10 minutes or until fish flakes easily with a fork. **Yield:** 4 servings.

Glazed Salmon Fillet

(Pictured above)

Jerilyn Colvin, Foxboro, Massachusetts

My husband caught a lot of salmon when we lived in Alaska, so I had to learn how to cook it. Basted with a sweet glaze, this tasty fillet is a staple in our house.

1-1/2 cups packed brown sugar
    6 tablespoons butter *or* margarine, melted
    3 to 6 tablespoons lemon juice
2-1/4 teaspoons dill weed
  3/4 teaspoon cayenne pepper
    1 salmon fillet (about 2 pounds)
Lemon-pepper seasoning

In a small bowl, combine the first five ingredients; mix well. Remove 1/2 cup to a saucepan; simmer until heated through. Set aside remaining mixture for basting.

Sprinkle salmon with lemon-pepper. Place on grill with skin side down. Grill, covered, over medium heat for 5 minutes. Brush with the reserved brown sugar mixture. Grill 10-15 minutes longer, basting occasionally, until fish flakes easily with a fork. Serve with the warmed sauce. **Yield:** 6-8 servings.

Grilled Salmon Steaks

(Pictured above)

Robert Bishop, Lexington, Kentucky

Salmon is a popular fish that's rich in nutrients. Seasoned with herbs and lemon juice, these flame-broiled steaks are excellent. Sprinkle the hot coals with rosemary for additional flavor or quickly prepare the entree indoors using your broiler.

✓ Uses less fat, sugar or salt. Includes Nutritional Analysis and Diabetic Exchanges.

  3 tablespoons dried rosemary, crushed, *divided*
  1 tablespoon rubbed sage
1/4 teaspoon white pepper
  1 tablespoon lemon juice
  1 tablespoon olive *or* canola oil
  6 salmon steaks (6 ounces *each*)

In a bowl, combine 4-1/2 teaspoons rosemary, sage, pepper, lemon juice and oil. Brush over both sides of salmon steaks. Coat grill rack with nonstick cooking spray before starting the grill. Sprinkle the remaining rosemary over hot coals for added flavor.

Place salmon on grill rack. Grill, covered, over medium heat for 5 minutes. Turn; grill 7-9 minutes longer or until fish flakes easily with a fork. **Yield:** 6 servings.

Nutritional Analysis: One serving equals 334 calories, 20 g fat (5 g saturated fat), 112 mg cholesterol, 81 mg sodium, 2 g carbohydrate, 1 g fiber, 34 g protein. **Diabetic Exchanges:** 5 lean meat, 1 fat.

Southwestern Catfish

(Pictured below)

Bruce Crittenden, Clinton, Mississippi

Catfish fillets are rubbed with a blend that includes chili powder, cumin, coriander, cayenne and paprika, then topped with homemade salsa. A green salad, garlic bread and baked sweet potatoes round out the meal nicely.

  3 medium tomatoes, chopped
1/4 cup chopped onion
  2 jalapeno peppers, seeded and finely chopped*
  2 tablespoons white wine vinegar *or* cider vinegar
  3 teaspoons salt, *divided*
  3 teaspoons paprika
  3 teaspoons chili powder
  1 to 1-1/2 teaspoons ground cumin
  1 to 1-1/2 teaspoons ground coriander
3/4 to 1 teaspoon cayenne pepper
1/2 teaspoon garlic powder
  4 catfish fillets (6 ounces *each*)

For salsa, in a bowl, combine the tomatoes, onion, jalapenos, vinegar and 1 teaspoon salt. Cover and refrigerate for at least 30 minutes.

Combine the paprika, chili powder, cumin, coriander, cayenne, garlic powder and remaining salt; rub over catfish. Coat grill rack with nonstick cooking

4 lettuce leaves
4 tomato slices

Brush both sides of fillets with lime juice; sprinkle with lemon-pepper. Coat grill rack with nonstick cooking spray before starting the grill. Grill fillets, covered, over medium heat for 5-6 minutes on each side or until fish flakes easily with a fork.

In a small bowl, combine the mayonnaise, mustard and honey. Spread over the bottom of each bun. Top with a fillet, lettuce and tomato; replace bun tops. **Yield:** 4 servings.

Nutritional Analysis: One sandwich (prepared with fat-free mayonnaise) equals 241 calories, 3 g fat (1 g saturated fat), 49 mg cholesterol, 528 mg sodium, 28 g carbohydrate, 2 g fiber, 24 g protein. **Diabetic Exchanges:** 3 very lean meat, 2 starch.

Spicy Bacon-Wrapped Shrimp

Jane Bone, Cape Coral, Florida

This recipe has been in our family for many years and always gets rave reviews. I combine tender marinated shrimp with bacon strips to produce these delightful appetizers that will surely disappear in a hurry.

1/4 cup sugar
1/4 cup lemon juice
  2 tablespoons olive *or* vegetable oil
  4 teaspoons paprika
  1 teaspoon *each* salt, pepper, curry powder, ground cumin and ground coriander
1/2 to 1 teaspoon cayenne pepper
 18 uncooked jumbo shrimp, peeled and deveined
  9 bacon strips, halved lengthwise

In a bowl, combine the sugar, lemon juice, oil and seasonings; mix well. Pour 1/4 cup marinade into a large resealable plastic bag; add the shrimp. Seal bag and turn to coat; refrigerate for 30-60 minutes. Cover and refrigerate remaining marinade for basting.

In a skillet, cook bacon over medium heat until cooked but not crisp. Drain on paper towels. Remove shrimp from marinade; discard the marinade. Wrap each shrimp with a piece of bacon and secure with a toothpick.

Grill bacon-wrapped shrimp, uncovered, over medium heat for 7-10 minutes or until shrimp turn pink, turning and basting with reserved marinade. **Yield:** 1-1/2 dozen.

spray before starting the grill. Grill fillets, uncovered, over medium heat for 5 minutes on each side or until fish flakes easily with a fork. Serve with salsa. **Yield:** 4 servings.

*Editor's Note: When cutting or seeding hot peppers, use rubber or plastic gloves to protect your hands. Avoid touching your face.

Grilled Fish Sandwiches

(Pictured above)

Violet Beard, Marshall, Illinois

I season fish fillets with lime juice and lemon-pepper before charbroiling them on the grill. A simple mayonnaise and honey-mustard sauce puts the sandwiches a step ahead of the rest.

 Uses less fat, sugar or salt. Includes Nutritional Analysis and Diabetic Exchanges.

  4 cod fillets (4 ounces *each*)
  1 tablespoon lime juice
1/2 teaspoon lemon-pepper seasoning
1/4 cup mayonnaise
  2 teaspoons Dijon mustard
  1 teaspoon honey
  4 hamburger buns, split

Sides
and
Breads

Grilled Corn and Peppers (p. 88)

Chapter 5

Eggplant Mexicano

Alyce de Roos, Sarnia, Ontario

Salsa gives fun flavor to eggplant slices in this speedy side dish. We had an overabundance of eggplant some years ago when this recipe caught my eye. My husband and I both think it's delicious.

> 1/2 cup vegetable oil
> 1 teaspoon garlic powder
> 1 teaspoon dried oregano
> 1 medium eggplant, peeled and cut into
>   1/2-inch slices
> 2/3 cup salsa, warmed
> 1/2 cup shredded Monterey Jack cheese

In a bowl, combine the oil, garlic powder and oregano; brush over both sides of eggplant. Grill, uncovered, over indirect medium heat for 2 minutes on each side or until tender. To serve, spoon a small amount of salsa into the center of each; sprinkle with cheese. **Yield:** 6 servings.

Grilled Potato Fans

(Pictured above)

Jennifer Black-Ortiz, San Jose, California

If you're looking for a change from plain baked potatoes, try these tender and buttery potato fans seasoned with oregano, garlic powder, celery and onion. To cut down on grilling time, I sometimes microwave the potatoes for 5-6 minutes before slicing them.

> 6 medium baking potatoes
> 2 medium onions, halved and thinly sliced
> 6 tablespoons butter *or* margarine, cubed
> 1/4 cup finely chopped celery
> 1 teaspoon salt
> 1 teaspoon dried oregano
> 1/4 teaspoon garlic powder
> 1/4 teaspoon pepper

With a sharp knife, make cuts 1/2 in. apart in each potato, leaving slices attached at the bottom. Fan the potatoes slightly. Place each on a piece of heavy-duty foil (about 12 in. square).

Insert onions and butter between potato slices. Sprinkle with celery, salt, oregano, garlic powder and pepper. Fold foil around potatoes and seal tightly. Grill, covered, over medium-hot heat for 40-45 minutes or until tender. **Yield:** 6 servings.

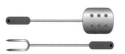

Veggies on the Grill

(Pictured below)

H. Ross Njaa, Salinas, California

I like to experiment a bit with marinades and sauces that combine different spices and herbs. This particular mix of seasonings really perks up garden-fresh vegetables.

> 1/3 cup vegetable oil
> 1-1/2 teaspoons garlic powder

1/2 teaspoon salt
1/4 teaspoon pepper
1/8 teaspoon cayenne pepper
3 medium carrots, halved lengthwise
3 large potatoes, quartered lengthwise
3 medium zucchini, quartered lengthwise

In a small bowl, combine oil, garlic powder, salt, pepper and cayenne. Brush over vegetables. Grill carrots and potatoes, covered, over medium heat for 10 minutes. Baste. Add zucchini. Cover and grill 10-15 minutes longer, basting and turning every 5 minutes or until vegetables are tender. **Yield:** 6 servings.

Cheddar Herb Bread

(Pictured at right)

Ann Jacobsen, Oakland, Michigan

This crunchy, delicious bread is a hit with my husband and children. It's a fun accompaniment to any meal you make on the grill—the garlic flavor really comes through.

1 cup (4 ounces) shredded cheddar cheese
1/2 cup butter *or* margarine, softened
1/4 cup minced fresh parsley
1 garlic clove, minced
1/2 teaspoon garlic powder
1/2 teaspoon paprika
1 loaf (1 pound) French bread, sliced

In a mixing bowl, combine the first six ingredients; beat until smooth. Spread on both sides of each slice of bread; reassemble the loaf. Wrap in a large piece of heavy-duty foil (about 28 in. x 18 in.); seal tightly. Grill, covered, over medium heat for 15-20 minutes or until heated through, turning once. **Yield:** 10-12 servings.

Editor's Note: Bread may also be heated in a 375° oven for 15-20 minutes.

Cabbage on the Grill

Demi Rice, Macks Creek, Missouri

My father first fixed these bacon-wrapped cabbage wedges a few years ago. Now I make them for my fami-ly when we put steak and potatoes on the grill. Even our three daughters like them.

1 medium head cabbage (about 2 pounds)
4 teaspoons butter *or* margarine, softened
1 teaspoon salt
1/2 teaspoon garlic powder
1/4 teaspoon pepper
2 tablespoons grated Parmesan cheese
4 bacon strips

Cut cabbage into four wedges; place each on a piece of double-layered heavy-duty foil (about 18 in. square). Spread cut sides with butter. Sprinkle with salt, garlic powder, pepper and Parmesan cheese. Wrap a bacon strip around each wedge.

Fold the foil around the cabbage and seal tightly. Grill, covered, over medium heat for 40 minutes or until the cabbage is tender, turning twice. **Yield:** 4 servings.

Utilizing Herbs

DRIED HERBS such as oregano, tarragon or rosemary sprinkled over hot coals just before grilling add fragrance and flavor to the food.

Grilled Three-Cheese Potatoes

(Pictured below)

Margaret Hanson-Maddox, Montpelier, Indiana

While this is delicious grilled, I've also cooked it in the oven at 350° for an hour. Add cubed ham to it and you can serve it as a full-meal main dish.

- 6 large potatoes, sliced 1/4 inch thick
- 2 medium onions, chopped
- 1/3 cup grated Parmesan cheese
- 1 cup (4 ounces) shredded sharp cheddar cheese, *divided*
- 1 cup (4 ounces) shredded mozzarella cheese, *divided*
- 1 pound sliced bacon, cooked and crumbled
- 1/4 cup butter *or* margarine, cubed
- 1 tablespoon minced fresh *or* dried chives
- 1 to 2 teaspoons seasoned salt
- 1/2 teaspoon pepper

Divide the potatoes and onions equally between two pieces of heavy-duty foil (about 18-in. square) that have been coated with nonstick cooking spray. Combine Parmesan cheese and 3/4 cup each cheddar and mozzarella; sprinkle over the potatoes and onions. Top with bacon, butter, chives, seasoned salt and pepper.

Bring opposite ends of foil together over filling and fold down several times. Fold unsealed ends toward

filling and crimp tightly. Grill, covered, over medium heat for 35-40 minutes or until potatoes are tender. Remove from the grill. Open foil carefully and sprinkle with remaining cheeses. **Yield:** 6-8 servings.

Colorful Grilled Veggies

(Pictured above)

Susan Jesson, Oro Station, Ontario

I put this combination together one day when trying to serve a side dish other than mushrooms in butter. Everyone loves this pleasantly seasoned medley.

 Uses less fat, sugar or salt. Includes Nutritional Analysis and Diabetic Exchanges.

- 10 cherry tomatoes, halved
- 2 celery ribs, thinly sliced
- 1 medium green pepper, sliced
- 1 medium sweet red pepper, sliced
- 1 medium red onion, sliced and separated into rings
- 1 cup sliced fresh mushrooms
- 1 tablespoon red wine vinegar *or* cider vinegar
- 1 tablespoon olive *or* canola oil
- 1 teaspoon lemon juice
- 1 garlic clove, minced
- 1 teaspoon dried basil

1/2 teaspoon salt
1/2 teaspoon pepper

Divide the vegetables between two pieces of heavy-duty foil (about 18 in. square). In a small bowl, combine the remaining ingredients; drizzle over vegetables. Fold foil around vegetables and seal tightly. Grill, covered, over medium heat for 10-15 minutes or until the vegetables are crisp-tender. **Yield:** 6 servings.
   Nutritional Analysis: One serving (3/4 cup) equals 51 calories, 3 g fat (trace saturated fat), 0 cholesterol, 212 mg sodium, 7 g carbohydrate, 2 g fiber, 1 g protein. **Diabetic Exchange:** 2 vegetable.

Sweet Onions with Radish Sauce

Phyllis Schmalz, Kansas City, Kansas

I stir up a light creamy sauce to complement sweet grilled onions. This side dish is a special treat in spring, when Vidalia onions are in season.

   2 large sweet onions, cut into 1/2-inch slices
1/4 cup olive *or* vegetable oil
1/2 teaspoon salt
1/8 teaspoon pepper
1/2 cup plain yogurt
   1 tablespoon mayonnaise
1/4 cup chopped radishes
   2 tablespoons snipped fresh dill *or* 2
      teaspoons dill weed

Brush both sides of onion slices with oil; sprinkle with salt and pepper. Place the onions directly on grill rack. Grill, covered, over indirect heat for 8 minutes on each side or until crisp-tender. In a small bowl, combine the yogurt, mayonnaise, radishes and dill. Serve with the onions. **Yield:** 4 servings.

Grilled Dijon Summer Squash

(Pictured at right)

Ruth Lee, Troy, Ontario

A niece gave this mustard-seasoned squash recipe to me. My husband, Doug, and our three grandchildren love the

zesty flavor and slightly crunchy texture. The kabobs are perfect partners to any grilled meat and reheat easily.

1/4 cup red wine vinegar *or* cider vinegar
   1 tablespoon minced fresh oregano
      or 1 teaspoon dried oregano
   1 tablespoon Dijon mustard
   2 garlic cloves, minced
1/2 teaspoon salt
1/4 teaspoon pepper
   4 medium zucchini, cut into 1/2-inch
      slices
   4 medium yellow squash, cut into 1/2-inch
      slices
   2 medium red onions, quartered
   1 large sweet red pepper, cut into 2-inch
      pieces
   1 large sweet yellow pepper, cut into 2-inch
      pieces
  12 to 16 whole fresh mushrooms
  12 cherry tomatoes

In a jar with a tight-fitting lid, combine the oil, vinegar, oregano, mustard, garlic, salt and pepper. Place the vegetables in a shallow baking dish. Add marinade and toss to coat. Let stand for 15 minutes.
   Drain and discard marinade; arrange vegetables on a vegetable grill rack. Grill, covered, over indirect heat for 10-12 minutes or until tender. **Yield:** 16-18 servings.

Grilled Corn and Peppers

(Pictured above and on page 82)

Cindy Williams, Fort Myers, Florida

Every Fourth of July, we invite family and friends to our houseboat for a cookout. We always have corn on the cob prepared this way, and everyone loves it. The onions and red and green peppers add fantastic flavor to the sweet ears of corn.

✓ Uses less fat, sugar or salt. Includes Nutritional Analysis and Diabetic Exchanges.

    3 cups Italian salad dressing
    8 large ears fresh corn, husked and cleaned
    4 medium green peppers, julienned
    4 medium sweet red peppers, julienned
    2 medium red onions, sliced and separated
      into rings

Place salad dressing in a large resealable plastic bag or shallow glass container. Add corn, peppers and onions; turn to coat. Seal or cover and refrigerate for 30 minutes.

Drain and discard marinade. Place vegetables in a grill pan or disposable foil pan with holes punched in the bottom. Grill, covered, over medium heat for 25 minutes or until corn is tender, turning frequently. **Yield:** 8 servings.

Nutritional Analysis: One serving (prepared with fat-free Italian dressing) equals 145 calories, 452 mg sodium, 0 cholesterol, 33 gm carbohydrate, 4 gm

protein, 1 gm fat, 5 gm fiber. **Diabetic Exchanges:** 1-1/2 starch, 1 vegetable.

Orange Vegetable Kabobs

(Pictured below)

Laurie Whitney, Bradford, Massachusetts

I created this recipe to add some zip to grilled vegetables. Their color, crispness and taste are tempting to all ages. Even my young son eats his veggies when I prepare them this way.

✓ Uses less fat, sugar or salt. Includes Nutritional Analysis and Diabetic Exchanges.

    1 large sweet onion
    1 large unpeeled navel orange
    1 medium sweet red pepper, cut into 1-inch
      pieces
    1 medium sweet yellow pepper, cut into
      1-inch pieces
    8 medium fresh mushrooms
    8 cherry tomatoes
    2 small yellow summer squash, cut into
      1-inch slices
MARINADE:
    1/2 cup olive *or* vegetable oil
    1/3 cup lemon juice
  1-1/2 teaspoons sugar

1 teaspoon salt, optional
1/4 teaspoon garlic powder
1/4 teaspoon pepper
2 tablespoons orange juice

Cut the onion and orange into eight wedges; halve each wedge. Alternately thread vegetables and orange pieces onto eight metal or soaked wooden skewers. Place in a shallow oblong dish. In a bowl, whisk together the oil, lemon juice, sugar, salt if desired, garlic powder and pepper. Pour over skewers. Marinate for 15 minutes, turning and basting frequently.

Grill, covered, over indirect heat for 10-15 minutes or until the vegetables are crisp-tender. Brush with orange juice just before serving. **Yield:** 8 kabobs.

Nutritional Analysis: One kabob (calculated without salt) equals 111 calories, 13 mg sodium, 0 cholesterol, 12 gm carbohydrate, 2 gm protein, 7 gm fat, 3 gm fiber. **Diabetic Exchanges:** 2 vegetable, 1 fat.

Rice on the Grill

Shirley Hopkins, Olds, Alberta

My husband loves to barbecue, so when it's hot outside, we do entire meals on the grill. Since our kids love rice, we often include this tangy side dish as part of the menu.

 Uses less fat, sugar or salt. Includes Nutritional Analysis and Diabetic Exchanges.

1-1/3 cups uncooked instant rice
1/3 cup sliced fresh mushrooms
1/4 cup chopped green pepper
1/4 cup chopped onion
1/2 cup chicken broth
1/2 cup water
1/3 cup ketchup
1 tablespoon butter *or* margarine

In a 9-in. round aluminum foil pie pan, combine the first seven ingredients. Dot with butter. Cover with heavy-duty foil; seal edges tightly. Grill, covered, for 14-15 minutes or until liquid is absorbed. Fluff with a fork and serve immediately. **Yield:** 6 servings.

Nutritional Analysis: One serving (prepared with reduced-sodium broth and reduced-fat margarine) equals 104 calories, 195 mg sodium, trace cholesterol, 21 gm carbohydrate, 2 gm protein, 2 gm fat, 1 gm fiber. **Diabetic Exchanges:** 1 starch, 1 vegetable.

Basil Garlic Bread

(Pictured above)

Stephanie Moon, Green Bay, Wisconsin

A must-have accompaniment for any grilled entree is this bread. Everyone loves it. It's easy and takes advantage of the already fired-up grill.

1/4 cup butter *or* margarine
2 tablespoons minced fresh parsley
1-1/2 teaspoons minced fresh basil *or* 1/2 teaspoon dried basil
1 garlic clove, minced
1/4 cup grated Parmesan cheese
1 loaf (8 ounces) French bread

In a microwave-safe bowl, combine butter, parsley, basil and garlic. Cover and microwave until butter is melted. Stir in Parmesan cheese. Cut the bread in half lengthwise; place cut side down on an uncovered grill over medium heat for 2 minutes. Brush cut side with the butter mixture. Grill 1-2 minutes longer. **Yield:** 4 servings.

Opening Foil Packets

OPEN FOIL packets cooked on the grill very cautiously to allow the steam to escape and to prevent burns.

Cookout Potatoes

Wanda Holoubek, Omaha, Nebraska

The recipe for this comforting potato side dish came from my mother. It's a snap to prepare with convenient frozen hash browns.

    4 cups cubed hash brown potatoes, thawed
    1/2 cup chopped celery
    1/2 cup chopped green pepper
    1/3 cup butter *or* margarine, melted
    2 tablespoons finely chopped onion
    1 tablespoon minced fresh parsley
    1 teaspoon salt

Combine all of the ingredients. Place on a double thickness of heavy-duty foil (about 28-in. x 18-in.). Fold foil around the potato mixture and seal tightly. Grill, covered, over medium heat for 45-50 minutes or until the potatoes are tender. **Yield:** 6-8 servings.

Grilled Garlic Bread

(Pictured below)

Priscilla Weaver, Hagerstown, Maryland

Until several years ago, I'd never thought of making garlic bread outdoors, but Grilled Garlic Bread turns out nice and crispy.

    1 loaf (16 ounces) French bread

    1/4 cup butter *or* margarine, softened
    1 teaspoon garlic powder

Cut the bread into eight slices. In a small bowl, combine the butter and garlic powder. Spread on one side of each slice of bread. Place bread, buttered side up, on a grill over medium heat for 2 minutes or until browned. Turn and grill 2 minutes longer or until browned. **Yield:** 8 servings.

Potato Floret Packet

(Pictured above)

Janet Hayes, Hermantown, Minnesota

This side dish was developed by my daughter, Betsey, who worked in a group home. When they would grill out, this attractive veggie medley was a favorite of the residents there.

 Uses less fat, sugar or salt. Includes Nutritional Analysis and Diabetic Exchanges.

    5 medium red potatoes, cubed
    1 cup fresh broccoli florets
    1 cup fresh cauliflowerets

1 small onion, chopped
1/4 teaspoon garlic salt *or* garlic powder
Pepper to taste
1/4 cup shredded cheddar cheese

In a bowl, combine the potatoes, broccoli, cauliflower, onion, garlic salt and pepper. Place on a double thickness of heavy-duty foil (about 17 in. x 12 in.). Fold foil around potato mixture and seal tightly.

Grill, covered, over medium heat for 30 minutes or until the potatoes are tender. Sprinkle with cheese before serving. **Yield:** 6 servings.

Nutritional Analysis: One 1-cup serving (prepared with garlic powder and reduced-fat cheese) equals 136 calories, 12 mg sodium, 1 mg cholesterol, 28 gm carbohydrate, 5 gm protein, 1 gm fat, 3 gm fiber. **Diabetic Exchanges:** 1-1/2 starch, 1 vegetable.

Bundle of Veggies

(Pictured below)

Sheila Dedman, New Dundee, Ontario

I came across the recipe for this grilled vegetable medley at a nurses' station at the hospital where I work. It's a big hit at home and while camping. The foil packet makes cleanup easy, too.

✓ Uses less fat, sugar or salt. Includes Nutritional Analysis and Diabetic Exchanges.

8 ounces whole fresh mushrooms
8 ounces cherry tomatoes
1 cup sliced zucchini
1 tablespoon olive *or* vegetable oil
1 tablespoon butter *or* margarine, melted
1/2 teaspoon salt *or* salt-free seasoning blend
1/2 teaspoon onion powder
1/2 teaspoon Italian seasoning
1/8 teaspoon garlic powder
Dash pepper

Place mushrooms, tomatoes and zucchini on a double thickness of heavy-duty foil (about 18 in. square). Combine the remaining ingredients; drizzle over vegetables. Fold the foil around vegetables and seal tightly. Grill, covered, over medium heat for 20-25 minutes or until tender. **Yield:** 6 servings.

Nutritional Analysis: One serving (prepared with reduced-fat margarine and salt-free seasoning) equals 52 calories, 27 mg sodium, 0 cholesterol, 5 gm carbohydrate, 1 gm protein, 4 gm fat. **Diabetic Exchanges:** 1 vegetable, 1/2 fat.

Oregano Onions

Marcia Preston, Clear Lake, Iowa

My dad, who loves onions, invented this tasty side dish. The tender seasoned onions go well with all types of grilled meat, so we enjoy them frequently, especially during the warm grilling season.

✓ Uses less fat, sugar or salt. Includes Nutritional Analysis and Diabetic Exchanges.

5 large onions, sliced
6 teaspoons butter *or* margarine
1-1/2 teaspoons dried oregano
Pepper to taste

Divide onions between two pieces of double-layered heavy-duty foil (about 22 in. x 18 in.) coated with nonstick cooking spray. Top each with butter, oregano and pepper. Fold foil around the mixture and seal tightly. Grill, covered, over indirect heat for 30-40 minutes or until onions are tender. **Yield:** 10 servings.

Nutritional Analysis: One serving (prepared with reduced-fat margarine) equals 41 calories, 28 mg sodium, 0 cholesterol, 7 gm carbohydrate, 1 gm protein, 2 gm fat. **Diabetic Exchanges:** 1 vegetable, 1/2 fat.

Harvest Vegetables

(Pictured above)

Linda Farni, Durango, Iowa

I wrap a lightly seasoned blend of veggies in foil for quick cooking. This colorful combination includes so many different vegetables that there's something to please everyone. Cleanup's a snap because there are no dishes to wash.

✓ Uses less fat, sugar or salt. Includes Nutritional Analysis and Diabetic Exchanges.

    1 small cabbage, cored
    2 tablespoons butter *or* margarine, softened
1/2 to 1 teaspoon onion salt, optional
1/8 to 1/4 teaspoon pepper
    4 medium carrots, cut into 1-inch pieces
    2 celery ribs, cut into 1-inch pieces
    1 small onion, cut into wedges
1/2 pound whole fresh mushrooms
    1 small green pepper, cut into pieces
    4 bacon strips, cooked and crumbled, optional

Cut cabbage into six wedges; spread butter on cut sides. Place cabbage on a piece of heavy-duty foil (about 24 in. x 18 in.). Sprinkle with onion salt if desired and pepper. Arrange the carrots, celery, onion, mushrooms, green pepper and bacon if desired around cabbage.

Seal the foil tightly. Grill, covered, over medium-hot heat for 30 minutes or until vegetables are tender, turning occasionally. **Yield:** 6 servings.

Nutritional Analysis: One serving (prepared with

margarine and without onion salt and bacon) equals 110 calories, 102 mg sodium, 0 cholesterol, 17 gm carbohydrate, 4 gm protein, 4 gm fat. **Diabetic Exchanges:** 1 starch, 1 fat.

Zucchini with Salsa

(Pictured below)

Carole Hildebrand, Kelseyville, California

I top zucchini slices with chunky homemade salsa to make this scrumptious side dish that cooks on the grill. I fix it often in the summer when I have the fresh vegetables on hand from my garden.

✓ Uses less fat, sugar or salt. Includes Nutritional Analysis and Diabetic Exchange.

    4 medium zucchini, sliced
    3 medium tomatoes, diced
    1 medium onion, diced
    3 green onions, sliced
    2 jalapeno peppers, seeded and minced*
    2 garlic cloves, minced
    1 tablespoon minced fresh cilantro
      or parsley
Salt and pepper to taste, optional

Divide zucchini between two pieces of heavy-duty foil (about 20 in. x 18 in.). In a bowl, combine the remaining ingredients; spoon over zucchini. Fold foil around vegetables and seal tightly. Grill, covered,

over indirect heat for 15-20 minutes or until vegetables are tender. **Yield:** 10 servings.

Nutritional Analysis: One 3/4-cup serving (prepared without salt) equals 26 calories, 7 mg sodium, 0 cholesterol, 6 gm carbohydrate, 1 gm protein, trace fat, 2 gm fiber. **Diabetic Exchange:** 1 vegetable.

***Editor's Note:** When cutting and seeding hot peppers, use rubber or plastic gloves to protect your hands. Avoid touching your face.

Red Potato Skewers

(Pictured above)

Dawn Finch, Prosser, Washington

As a busy mother of three boys, I love to find good grilling recipes that my husband can use. A seasoned mayonnaise mixture keeps these quartered potatoes moist and heavenly.

 Uses less fat, sugar or salt. Includes Nutritional Analysis and Diabetic Exchange.

    2 pounds red potatoes (about 6 medium),
      quartered
1/2 cup water
1/2 cup mayonnaise *or* salad dressing
1/4 cup chicken broth
    2 teaspoons dried oregano
1/2 teaspoon garlic salt
1/2 teaspoon onion powder

Place the potatoes and water in an ungreased microwave-safe 2-qt. dish. Cover and microwave on

high for 12-14 minutes, stirring once; drain. Combine remaining ingredients in a bowl; add potatoes. Cover and refrigerate for 1 hour.

Drain, reserving mayonnaise mixture. Thread the potatoes onto metal or soaked wooden skewers. Grill, uncovered, over medium heat for 4 minutes. Turn; brush with reserved mayonnaise mixture. Grill 4 minutes longer or until golden brown. **Yield:** 6 servings.

Nutritional Analysis: One serving (prepared with reduced-sodium broth and reduced-fat mayonnaise) equals 167 calories, 307 mg sodium, trace cholesterol, 21 gm carbohydrate, 4 gm protein, 7 gm fat. **Diabetic Exchanges:** 1-1/2 starch, 1-1/2 fat.

Editor's Note: This recipe was tested in an 850-watt microwave.

Grilled Sweet Corn

Connie Lou Hollister, Lake Odessa, Michigan

Since we have plenty of fresh sweet corn available in our area, we use this recipe often during summer months. Parsley, chili powder and cumin accent the corn's just-picked flavor.

    8 large ears sweet corn in husks
    6 tablespoons butter *or* margarine, softened
    1 tablespoon minced fresh parsley
    1 to 2 teaspoons chili powder
    1 teaspoon garlic salt
1/2 to 1 teaspoon ground cumin

Carefully peel back husks from corn to within 1 in. of bottom; remove silk. Combine remaining ingredients; spread over corn. Rewrap corn in husks and secure with string. Place in a large kettle; cover with cold water. Soak for 20 minutes; drain.

Grill the corn, covered, over medium heat for 10-15 minutes or until tender, turning often. **Yield:** 8 servings.

Time-Pressed Tip

IF YOU'RE SHORT on time, give meats and dense vegetables, like potatoes, a jump-start by cooking them halfway done in the microwave oven. Then you can finish cooking them on the grill.

Grilled food will cook more evenly if there's about 3/4 inch between pieces.

Lemon Garlic Mushrooms

(Pictured at right)

Diane Hixon, Niceville, Florida

I baste whole mushrooms with a lemony sauce to prepare this simple side dish. Using skewers or a grill basket makes it easy to turn these mushrooms.

☑ Uses less fat, sugar or salt. Includes Nutritional Analysis and Diabetic Exchanges.

   1/4 cup lemon juice
     3 tablespoons minced fresh parsley
     2 tablespoons olive *or* vegetable oil
     3 garlic cloves, minced
Pepper to taste
     1 pound large fresh mushrooms

In a small bowl, combine the first five ingredients; set aside. Grill mushrooms, covered, over medium-hot heat for 5 minutes. Brush generously with lemon mixture. Turn mushrooms; grill 5-8 minutes longer or until tender. Brush with remaining lemon mixture before serving. **Yield:** 4 servings.

    Nutritional Analysis: One serving equals 96 calories, 7 mg sodium, 0 cholesterol, 8 gm carbohydrate, 3 gm protein, 7 gm fat, 2 gm fiber. **Diabetic Exchanges:** 1-1/2 fat, 1 vegetable.

Grilled Cheese Loaf

(Pictured below left and on front cover)

Debbi Baker, Green Springs, Ohio

Generally, I like to serve this cheesy bread with steaks and salads. The loaf's so quick to make, in fact, I often grill two of them at a time.

     1 package (3 ounces) cream cheese, softened
     2 tablespoons butter *or* margarine, softened
     1 cup (4 ounces) shredded mozzarella cheese
   1/4 cup chopped green onions with tops
   1/2 teaspoon garlic salt
     1 loaf (1 pound) French bread, sliced

In a mixing bowl, beat cream cheese and butter. Add mozzarella, onions and garlic salt; mix well. Spread on both sides of each slice of bread. Wrap loaf in a large piece of heavy-duty foil (about 28 in. x 18 in.); seal tightly. Grill, covered, over medium heat for 8-10 minutes, turning once. Unwrap foil; grill 5 minutes longer. **Yield:** 10-12 servings.

Grilled Jalapenos

Catherine Hollie, Cleveland, Texas

When barbecuing with friends, I use the grill to serve up these zesty stuffed peppers. These crowd-pleasing bites have a bit of a kick. The recipe was concocted by my son, who loves to cook as well.

24 fresh jalapeno peppers
12 ounces bulk pork sausage
12 bacon strips, halved

Wash peppers and remove stems. Cut a slit along one side of each pepper. Remove seeds; rinse and dry peppers.

In a skillet over medium heat, cook sausage until no longer pink; drain. Stuff peppers with sausage and wrap with bacon; secure with a toothpick.

On an uncovered grill over medium heat, grill peppers for about 15 minutes or until tender and bacon is crisp, turning frequently. **Yield:** 2 dozen.

Editor's Note: When cutting and seeding hot peppers, use rubber or plastic gloves to protect your hands. Avoid touching your face.

Snappy Peas 'n' Mushrooms

(Pictured below)

Laura Mahaffey, Annapolis, Maryland

I make this delightful dill-seasoned dish in mere minutes. Just wrap the fresh vegetables in foil, seal tightly and grill until tender. It's that easy.

1 pound fresh sugar snap *or* snow peas
1/2 cup sliced fresh mushrooms

2 tablespoons sliced green onions
1 tablespoon snipped fresh dill *or* 1 teaspoon dill weed
2 tablespoons butter *or* margarine
Salt and pepper to taste

Place peas and mushrooms on a piece of double-layered heavy-duty foil (about 18 in. square). Sprinkle with onions and dill; dot with butter. Fold foil around the mixture and seal tightly.

Grill, covered, over medium-hot heat for 5 minutes. Turn; grill 5-8 minutes longer or until the vegetables are tender. Season with salt and pepper. **Yield:** 8-10 servings.

Grilled Onion Potatoes

Janet Gioia, Broadalbin, New York

When we were growing up, my mother often fixed these potatoes when we grilled outdoors during the warm summer months. The tasty treatment requires just a few ingredients, so you can have them sizzling on the grill in no time at all.

5 medium baking potatoes
1 small onion, sliced
Salt and pepper to taste
1 bottle (8 ounces) zesty Italian salad dressing

Cut each potato into five slices. Place onion between slices and sprinkle with salt and pepper. Reassemble each potato; place on a double layer of heavy-duty foil (about 12 in. square).

Pour about 2-4 tablespoons of salad dressing over each potato. Wrap foil around the potatoes and seal tightly. Grill, covered, over medium heat for 50-60 minutes or until the potatoes are tender. **Yield:** 5 servings.

Keep It Clean

BAKING PANS clean up easily after grilling if they are completely covered with aluminum foil first. When done cooking and the pan has cooled, just remove the foil and discard.

Grilled Veggie Mix

(Pictured above)

Janet Boulger, Botwood, Newfoundland

Living on this beautiful Canadian island, we often grill out so we can eat while enjoying the scenery. This tempting veggie dish is the perfect accompaniment to any barbecue fare. To make the recipe even more satisfying, I often use my homegrown vegetables and herbs in the mix.

    2 medium zucchini, cut into 1/2-inch slices
    1 large green pepper, cut into 1/2-inch
       squares
    1 large sweet red pepper, cut into 1/2-inch
       squares
    1 pound fresh mushrooms, halved
    1 large onion, cubed
    6 medium carrots, cut into 1/4-inch slices
    2 cups small broccoli florets
    2 cups small cauliflowerets
DRESSING:
    1/4 cup olive *or* vegetable oil
    1/4 cup butter *or* margarine, melted
    1/4 cup minced fresh parsley
    2 garlic cloves, minced
    1 teaspoon dried basil
    1/2 teaspoon dried oregano
    1/2 teaspoon salt
    1/4 teaspoon pepper

Place all of the the vegetables in the center of two pieces of double-layered heavy-duty foil (about 18 in. square). Combine all of the dressing ingredients; drizzle over vegetables. Fold foil around mixture and seal tightly. Grill, covered, over medium heat for 30 minutes or until vegetables are tender, turning once. **Yield:** 10 servings.

Grilled Vegetable Potato Skins

(Pictured below)

Karen Hemminger, Mansfield, Massachusetts

People just love these stuffed spuds in the summer as an alternative to heavier grilled fare. Topped with a colorful vegetable medley, the tender potato skins are light yet satisfying.

✓ Uses less fat, sugar or salt. Includes Nutritional Analysis and Diabetic Exchanges.

    2 large baking potatoes
    1 cup sliced yellow summer squash
    1 cup sliced zucchini
 1/2 large sweet red pepper, julienned

1/2 large green pepper, julienned
1 small red onion, cut into 1/4-inch wedges
1/4 cup reduced-fat olive oil and vinegar salad
    dressing *or* Italian salad dressing
1-1/2 teaspoons olive *or* canola oil
1/2 teaspoon salt, *divided*
1/4 cup shredded reduced-fat cheddar cheese

Pierce potatoes several times with a fork and place on a microwave-safe plate. Microwave on high for 18-20 minutes or until tender, rotating the potatoes once. Let stand until cool enough to handle.

Meanwhile, in a large resealable plastic bag, combine the summer squash, zucchini, peppers and onion. Pour salad dressing over vegetables. Seal bag and turn to coat; marinate for 20 minutes.

Cut each potato in half lengthwise. Scoop out pulp, leaving a thin shell (discard pulp or save for another use). Brush inside of shells with oil and sprinkle with 1/4 teaspoon salt.

Coat grill rack with nonstick cooking spray. Place potato shells skin side up on grill rack. Grill, covered, over indirect medium heat for 10 minutes or until golden brown.

Drain vegetables, reserving marinade. Grill vegetables in a grill basket, uncovered, over medium heat for 10 minutes or until tender, basting with reserved marinade.

Sprinkle potato skins with cheese. Fill with grilled vegetables; sprinkle with remaining salt. Grill 5 minutes longer or until cheese is melted. **Yield:** 4 servings.

Nutritional Analysis: One serving (1 stuffed potato half) equals 107 calories, 6 g fat (2 g saturated fat), 4 mg cholesterol, 497 mg sodium, 11 g carbohydrate, 3 g fiber, 4 g protein. **Diabetic Exchanges:** 1 vegetable, 1 fat, 1/2 starch.

Editor's Note: This recipe was tested in an 850-watt microwave.

6 medium ears sweet corn
1/2 cup butter *or* margarine, melted
2 tablespoons Dijon mustard
1 tablespoon minced fresh parsley
2 teaspoons prepared horseradish
1/2 teaspoon salt
1/4 teaspoon pepper

Place ears of corn on a double thickness of heavy-duty foil. In a small bowl, combine the remaining ingredients; brush over corn. Fold foil around corn and seal tightly. Grill, covered, over medium heat for 25-30 minutes or until corn is tender, turning once. **Yield:** 6 servings.

Zippy Corn on the Cob

(Pictured above right)

Barb Sass, Burton, Ohio

Dijon mustard and horseradish perk up this summertime favorite. You can prepare this sweet corn on the grill or in the oven. I can't remember where I found this recipe, but it's a real keeper! I serve it often, much to my family's delight.

A Kernel About Corn

HERE'S ANOTHER WAY to cook corn on the grill. To grill corn, remove the silk but leave the husks; use a metal twist tie to close the husks at the top. Soak the corn in cold water for 15 minutes so the husks don't burn while grilling. Grill for 15 to 30 minutes, turning frequently, depending on the size of the ear.

Remove the kernels from leftover cooled corn on the cob and use in soups, salads— you name it!

Grilled Peppers and Zucchini

(Pictured below)

Karen Anderson, Fair Oaks, California

This versatile side dish is so simple and quick that I had to share it. Grilling the colorful veggies in a foil packet means one less dish to wash, but I often stir-fry the mixture on the stovetop instead.

> 1 medium green pepper, julienned
> 1 medium sweet red pepper, julienned
> 2 medium zucchini, julienned
> 1 tablespoon butter *or* margarine
> 2 teaspoons soy sauce

Place the vegetables on a double layer of heavy-duty foil (about 18 in. x 15 in.). Dot with butter; drizzle with soy sauce. Fold foil around vegetables and seal tightly. Grill, covered, over medium heat for 10-15 minutes or until vegetables are crisp-tender. **Yield:** 3-4 servings.

Grilled Sweet Potatoes

(Pictured above right)

Lillian Neer, Long Eddy, New York

I love trying new recipes, so when my son-in-law suggested we grill sweet potatoes, I said yes. Served with steak, they're a great change of pace from traditional baked potatoes...and pretty, too.

 Uses less fat, sugar or salt. Includes Nutritional Analysis and Diabetic Exchanges.

> 2 large sweet potatoes, halved lengthwise
> 2 tablespoons butter *or* margarine, softened
> Garlic salt and pepper to taste
> 2 teaspoons honey

Cut two pieces of heavy-duty foil (about 18 in. x 12 in.); place a potato half on each. Spread cut side with butter. Sprinkle with garlic salt and pepper. Top each potato with another half.

Fold foil over potatoes and seal tightly. Grill, covered, over medium-hot heat for 30 minutes or until tender, turning once. To serve, fluff potatoes with a fork and drizzle with honey. **Yield:** 4 servings.

Nutritional Analysis: One serving (prepared with margarine and without garlic salt) equals 123 calories, 73 mg sodium, 0 cholesterol, 16 gm carbohydrate, 1 gm protein, 6 gm fat. **Diabetic Exchanges:** 1 starch, 1 fat.

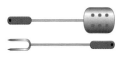

Barbecued Olive Bread

Patricia Gasper, Peoria, Illinois

We cook on the grill all year long, so this zesty olive-topped bread accompanies everything from pork to beef to chicken. It's a nice change of pace from serving garlic bread that also makes a tempting appetizer.

1 can (4-1/2 ounces) chopped ripe olives, drained
1/2 cup chopped stuffed olives
3/4 cup shredded Colby/Monterey Jack cheese
3/4 cup grated Parmesan cheese, *divided*
1/4 cup butter *or* margarine, melted
1 tablespoon olive *or* vegetable oil
2 garlic cloves, minced
3 drops hot pepper sauce
2 cups biscuit/baking mix
2/3 cup milk
2 tablespoons minced fresh parsley
Paprika

In a bowl, combine the olives, Colby/Monterey Jack cheese, 1/2 cup Parmesan cheese, butter, oil, garlic and hot pepper sauce; set aside. In another bowl, combine biscuit mix, milk, 2 tablespoons Parmesan cheese and parsley just until moistened. Press into two greased 9-in. disposable aluminum pie pans. Top with olive mixture; sprinkle with paprika and remaining Parmesan.

Grill bread, covered, over indirect heat for 8-10 minutes or until bottom crust is golden brown when edge of bread is lifted with a spatula. **Yield:** 2 loaves (6-8 servings each).

Pesto-Corn Grilled Peppers

(Pictured above right)

Rachael Marrier, Star Prairie, Wisconsin

We grill almost daily and enjoy using fresh produce from our garden. These pepper halves filled with a basil-seasoned corn mixture is my husband's favorite.

1/2 cup plus 2 teaspoons olive *or* vegetable oil, *divided*
3/4 cup grated Parmesan cheese
2 cups tightly packed fresh basil
2 tablespoons sunflower kernels *or* walnuts
4 garlic cloves
1/2 cup finely chopped sweet red pepper
4 cups whole kernel corn
4 medium sweet red, yellow *or* green peppers
1/4 cup shredded Parmesan cheese, optional

For pesto, combine 1/2 cup of oil, grated Parmesan cheese, basil, sunflower kernels and garlic in a blend-er or food processor; cover and process until blended. In a skillet, saute red pepper in remaining oil until tender. Add corn and pesto; heat through.

Halve peppers lengthwise; remove seeds. Place, cut side down, on grill over medium heat; cover and cook for 8 minutes. Turn; fill with corn mixture. Grill 4-6 minutes longer or until tender. Sprinkle with shredded Parmesan cheese if desired. **Yield:** 8 servings.

Grilled Cherry Tomatoes

Lucy Meyring, Walden, Colorado

Seasoned with herbs and butter, these tomatoes make a colorful and tasty side dish. Just tuck the foil packet beside any meat you happen to be grilling.

2 pints cherry tomatoes, halved
2 garlic cloves, minced
1/2 teaspoon dried oregano
3 tablespoons butter *or* margarine

Place tomatoes on a double thickness of heavy-duty foil (about 24 in. x 12 in.). In a skillet, saute garlic and oregano in butter for 2 minutes. Pour over tomatoes. Fold foil around tomatoes and seal tightly.

Grill, covered, over medium heat for 8-10 minutes or until the tomatoes are heated through, turning once. **Yield:** 4-6 servings.

Artichoke Mushroom Caps

(Pictured below)

Ruth Lewis, West Newton, Pennsylvania

These crumb-topped appetizers never last long at our get-togethers. The rich filling of cream cheese, artichoke hearts, Parmesan cheese and green onion is terrific. You can broil them in your oven to enjoy any time of year.

> 1 package (3 ounces) cream cheese, softened
> 1/4 cup mayonnaise
> 1 jar (6-1/2 ounces) marinated artichoke hearts, drained and finely chopped
> 1/4 cup grated Parmesan cheese
> 2 tablespoons finely chopped green onion
> 20 to 25 large fresh mushrooms, stems removed
> 1/4 cup seasoned bread crumbs
> 2 teaspoons olive *or* vegetable oil

In a mixing bowl, beat cream cheese and mayonnaise until smooth. Beat in the artichokes, Parmesan cheese and onion. Lightly spray tops of mushrooms with non-stick cooking spray. Spoon cheese mixture into mushroom caps. Combine bread crumbs and oil; sprinkle over mushrooms.

Grill, covered, over indirect medium heat for 8-10 minutes or until mushrooms are tender. **Yield:** about 2 dozen.

Summer Vegetable Medley

(Pictured above)

Maria Regakis, Somerville, Massachusetts

This swift side dish is as beautiful as it is delicious. Red and yellow peppers, zucchini, corn and mush-rooms are seasoned with garden-fresh herbs. Grilled in a foil pan, it's no-fuss cooking.

> 1/2 cup butter *or* margarine, melted
> 1-1/4 teaspoons *each* minced fresh parsley, basil and chives
> 3/4 teaspoon salt
> 1/4 teaspoon pepper
> 3 medium ears sweet corn, husks removed, cut into 2-inch pieces
> 1 medium sweet red pepper, cut into 1-inch pieces
> 1 medium sweet yellow pepper, cut into 1-inch pieces
> 1 medium zucchini, cut into 1/4-inch slices
> 10 large fresh mushrooms

In a large bowl, combine the butter, parsley, basil, chives, salt and pepper. Add the vegetables; toss to coat. Place vegetables in a disposable foil pan. Grill, covered, over medium-high heat for 5 minutes; stir. Grill 5 minutes longer or until the vegetables are tender. **Yield:** 6-8 servings.

Grilled Hash Browns

(Pictured above)

Kelly Chastain, Bedford, Indiana

Since my husband and I love to grill meats, we're always looking for easy side dishes that cook on the grill, too. So I came up with this simple recipe for hash browns.

3-1/2 cups frozen cubed hash brown potatoes, thawed
1 small onion, chopped
1 tablespoon beef bouillon granules
Dash *each* seasoned salt and pepper
1 tablespoon butter *or* margarine, melted

Place potatoes on a piece of heavy-duty foil (20 in. x 18 in.) coated with cooking spray. Sprinkle with onion, bouillon, salt and pepper; drizzle with butter.

Fold foil around potatoes; seal tightly. Grill, covered, over indirect medium heat for 10-15 minutes until potatoes are tender, turning once. **Yield:** 4 servings.

Summer Squash Bundles

Juanita Daugherty, Cadet, Missouri

We love zucchini, and my husband enjoys cooking summer meals on the grill, so I came up with this idea to add to our outdoor dining menu.

1 green onion
1 medium yellow squash
1 medium zucchini
1/4 cup chopped leek (white portion only)
2 tablespoons grated Parmesan cheese
2 teaspoons Italian seasoning
2 teaspoons butter *or* margarine, melted
1/4 teaspoon salt

Remove white portion of green onion (save for another use). Trim the onion top to 8- or 9-in. lengths. In a saucepan, bring water to a boil. Add onion tops; boil for 1 minute or until softened. Drain and immediately place in ice water. Drain and pat dry; set aside.

Cut squash and zucchini in half lengthwise. Scoop out pulp from zucchini halves, leaving a 3/8-in. shell. Discard pulp. In a bowl, combine the remaining ingredients; fill zucchini shells. Place yellow squash halves, cut side down, over filled zucchini halves. Tie each bundle with a blanched onion top.

Wrap each bundle in a double thickness of heavy-duty foil (12 in. square). Fold foil around squash and seal tightly. Grill, covered, over medium heat for 15-20 minutes or until tender. **Yield:** 2 servings.

Open Fire Bread

Kathy Thye Dewbre, Kimberley, South Africa

My husband and I have been missionaries in Africa for years. We were introduced to this bread at a street fair, where it was cooked over an open fire.

2 packages (1/4 ounce *each*) active dry yeast
2 teaspoons honey
3 cups warm water (110° to 115°), *divided*
2 teaspoons salt
1 tablespoon vegetable oil
7 to 8 cups all-purpose flour

In a mixing bowl, combine yeast, honey and 2/3 cup water; mix well. Let stand 5 minutes. Add salt, oil, remaining water and 6 cups flour; mix well. Add enough remaining flour to form a soft dough. Turn onto a floured surface; knead until smooth and elastic, about 6-8 minutes. (Dough will be soft and slightly sticky.) Place in a greased bowl, turning once to grease top. Cover and let rise in a warm place until doubled, about 1 hour.

Punch dough down. On a floured surface, roll out dough to 3/4-in. thickness. Cut into 4-in. x 1-in. strips with a pizza cutter; sprinkle with flour. Place on a floured baking sheet. Let rise until doubled, about 25-30 minutes. Place strips directly on grill. Grill, uncovered, over medium-hot heat until golden brown, about 6-8 minutes, turning often. **Yield:** about 3 dozen.

Sweet
Treats

Grilled Peaches with Berry Sauce (p. 107)

Chapter 6

Grilled Fruit Kabobs

(Pictured above)

Mrs. Travis Baker, Litchfield, Illinois

Instead of making a traditional fruit salad, why not try these quick-and-easy kabobs? They cook on the grill in a matter of minutes, so you'll have a refreshingly fruit dessert in no time. Plus, they're fun to eat!

　1/2 fresh pineapple, trimmed and cut into
　　　1-inch chunks
　　3 medium fresh nectarines, cut into 1-inch
　　　chunks
　　3 medium fresh pears, cut into 1-inch chunks
　　3 medium fresh peaches, cut into 1-inch
　　　chunks
　　3 to 4 plums, cut into 1-inch chunks
　　10 apricots, halved
Honey *or* corn syrup

Thread the pineapple, nectarines, pears, peaches, plums and apricots alternately onto metal or soaked wooden skewers. Grill, uncovered, over medium-hot heat until fruit is heated through, about 6 minutes, turning often. Brush with honey or corn syrup during the last minute of grilling time. **Yield:** 4-6 servings.

Cinnamon Flat Rolls

Ethel Farnsworth, Yuma, Arizona

I shared this recipe when 4-H leaders requested an activity for younger members. The kids had a ball rolling out the dough and enjoying the sweet chewy results.

　　1 package (16 ounces) frozen dinner rolls,
　　　thawed
　　5 tablespoons vegetable oil
　1/2 cup sugar
　　1 tablespoon ground cinnamon

On a floured surface, roll each dinner roll into a 5-in. circle. Brush with oil. Grill, uncovered, over medium heat for 1 minute on each side or until golden brown (burst any large bubbles with a fork). Combine sugar and cinnamon; sprinkle over rolls. **Yield:** 1 dozen.

Cookout Caramel S'mores

(Pictured below)

Martha Haseman, Hinckley, Illinois

These tasty treats make a great finish to an informal meal. Toasting the marshmallows extends our after-dinner time together, giving us something fun to do as a family. Plus, they're a sweet reward to us all for eating healthier.

 Uses less fat, sugar or salt. Includes Nutritional Analysis and Diabetic Exchanges.

8 large marshmallows
2 teaspoons fat-free chocolate syrup
8 reduced-fat graham crackers (2-1/2-inch square)
2 teaspoons fat-free caramel ice cream topping

Using a long-handled fork, toast marshmallows 6 in. from medium-hot heat until golden brown, turning occasionally. Drizzle chocolate syrup over four graham crackers; top each with two toasted marshmallows. Drizzle with caramel topping. Cover with remaining graham crackers. **Yield:** 4 servings.

Nutritional Analysis: One serving equals 87 calories, trace fat (trace saturated fat), trace cholesterol, 82 mg sodium, 20 g carbohydrate, trace fiber, 1 g protein. **Diabetic Exchange:** 1 starch.

Dessert from the Grill

(Pictured above right)

Becky Gillespie, Boulder, Colorado

I complete a grilled meal with this light, refreshing dessert. By the time we're done eating, the coals have cooled to the right temperature. I brush slices of pineapple and pound cake with a sweet sauce, toast them on the grill and top 'em with ice cream and convenient caramel sauce.

1 can (20 ounces) sliced pineapple
1 tablespoon butter *or* margarine
1/2 teaspoon brown sugar
1/4 teaspoon vanilla extract
1/8 teaspoon ground cinnamon
1/8 teaspoon ground nutmeg
6 slices pound cake
Vanilla ice cream
Caramel ice cream topping

Drain pineapple, reserving 1/3 cup juice and six pineapple rings (save remaining juice and pineapple for another use). In a microwave-safe dish, combine butter, brown sugar, vanilla, cinnamon, nutmeg and reserved pineapple juice.

Microwave, uncovered, on high for 1-2 minutes or until bubbly. Brush half of the mixture on both sides of pineapple rings and cake slices. On an uncovered grill over medium heat, cook pineapple and cake for 1-2 minutes on each side or until golden brown, brushing occasionally with remaining pineapple juice

mixture. Top each slice of cake with a pineapple ring and scoop of ice cream; drizzle with caramel topping. Serve immediately. **Yield:** 6 servings.

Banana Boats

Sandy Vanderhoff, Waldron, Arkansas

When I was a church youth leader, I introduced many young campers to this scrumptious treat. It's wonderful because each person can add their choice of yummy toppings to this warm dessert. They taste almost like banana splits.

4 medium unpeeled ripe bananas
2 tablespoons flaked coconut
2 tablespoons chopped maraschino cherries
2 tablespoons raisins
2 tablespoons peanut butter chips
1/2 cup miniature marshmallows

Cut banana peels lengthwise about 1/2 in. deep and to within 1/2 in. of each end. Open peel to form a pocket. Combine coconut and cherries; spoon into pockets of two bananas. Combine raisins and peanut butter chips; fill remaining bananas. Divide marshmallows between bananas. Wrap each in an 18-in. x 12-in. piece of heavy-duty foil.

Grill, uncovered, over medium heat for 10-15 minutes or until marshmallows are melted and golden brown. **Yield:** 4 servings.

Grilled Pineapple

(Pictured below)

Polly Heer, Cabot, Arkansas

Fresh pineapple adds an elegant touch to a barbecue when grilled, topped with butter and maple syrup and sprinkled with nuts. I suggest cutting each pineapple quarter into bite-size pieces before serving.

- 1/4 cup maple syrup
- 3 tablespoons butter (no substitutes), melted
- 1 fresh pineapple
- 2 tablespoons chopped macadamia nuts *or* hazelnuts, toasted

Combine syrup and butter; set aside. Quarter the pineapple lengthwise, leaving top attached. Grill, uncovered, over medium heat for 5 minutes. Turn; brush with maple butter. Grill 5-7 minutes longer or until heated through; brush with maple butter and sprinkle with nuts. Serve with remaining maple butter. **Yield:** 4 servings.

Chocolate Dessert Wraps

(Pictured above right)

Laurie Gwaltney, Indianapolis, Indiana

I came up with this chocolate and peanut butter treat when I needed a unique, fast dessert for a special din-

ner. The filled tortillas take just minutes on the grill and get a chewy consistency from marshmallows.

- 1/2 cup creamy peanut butter*
- 4 flour tortillas (8 inches)
- 1 cup miniature marshmallows
- 1/2 cup miniature semisweet chocolate chips

Vanilla ice cream
Chocolate shavings, optional

Spread 2 tablespoons of peanut butter on each tortilla. Sprinkle 1/4 cup marshmallows and 2 tablespoons chocolate chips on half of each tortilla. Roll up, beginning with the topping side. Wrap each tortilla in heavy-duty foil; seal tightly.

Grill, covered, over low heat for 5-10 minutes or until heated through. Unwrap tortillas and place on dessert plates. Serve with ice cream. Garnish with chocolate shavings if desired. **Yield:** 4 servings.

*Editor's Note: Crunchy peanut butter is not recommended for this recipe.

Red-Hot Apples

Helen Shubert, Hays, Kansas

I use red-hot candies to turn ordinary apples into something cinnamony and sensational. The tender treats bake on the grill during dinner.

4 medium tart apples, cored
4 teaspoons brown sugar
1/4 cup red-hot candies
Vanilla ice cream, optional

Place each apple in the center of a piece of heavy-duty foil (12 in. square). Spoon 1 teaspoon sugar and 1 tablespoon red-hots into the center of each apple. Fold foil around apple and seal tightly.

Grill, covered, over medium-hot heat for 30 minutes or until apples are tender. Carefully transfer apples and syrup to bowls. Serve warm with ice cream if desired. **Yield:** 4 servings.

Baked Apples on the Grill

Jodi Rugg, Aurora, Illinois

Sweet flaked coconut provides the delicious difference in this fun grilled treat. Our two young children enjoy helping me stuff the yummy filling into the apples. It's so easy to do that sometimes we don't even bother to do the measuring!

4 medium tart apples, cored
1/3 cup raisins
1/3 cup flaked coconut
1/4 cup packed brown sugar
1/2 teaspoon ground cinnamon

Place each apple on a 12-in. square piece of heavy-duty foil. Combine all of the remaining ingredients; spoon into the center of apples. Fold foil over the apples and seal tightly. Grill, covered, over medium heat for 20-25 minutes or until the apples are tender. **Yield:** 4 servings.

Preparing Fruit

WASH FRUIT just before use under cool, running water—use a vegetable brush if necessary. Remove any blemished areas.

Removing pits from fruits like peaches or nectarines is easier if you cut the fruit from stem to stem all the way to the stone. Twist the halves in opposite directions and lift out the pit.

Grilled Peaches with Berry Sauce

(Pictured below and on page 102)

Nancy Johnson, Connersville, Indiana

This unusual dessert is as pretty as it is delicious. Topped with brown sugar and cinnamon, the peaches come off the grill sweet and spicy. The raspberry sauce adds a refreshing touch.

1/2 of a 10-ounce package frozen raspberries in syrup, slightly thawed
1-1/2 teaspoons lemon juice
2 medium fresh peaches, peeled and halved
5 teaspoons brown sugar
1/4 teaspoon ground cinnamon
1/2 teaspoon vanilla extract
1 teaspoon butter *or* margarine

In a blender or food processor, process raspberries and lemon juice until pureed. Strain and discard seeds. Cover and chill.

Place the peach halves, cut side up, on a large piece of heavy-duty foil (about 18 in. x 12 in.). Combine brown sugar and cinnamon; sprinkle into peach centers. Sprinkle with vanilla; dot with butter. Fold foil over peaches and seal.

Grill over medium-hot heat for 15 minutes or until heated through. To serve, spoon the raspberry sauce over peaches. **Yield:** 4 servings.

General Recipe Index

✓ Recipe includes Nutritional Analysis and Diabetic Exchanges.

✓ Recipe includes Nutritional Analysis and Diabetic Exchanges.

✓ Recipe includes Nutritional Analysis and Diabetic Exchanges.

✓ Recipe includes Nutritional Analysis and Diabetic Exchanges.

✓ Recipe includes Nutritional Analysis and Diabetic Exchanges.